Emotional Eating

An Effective Step by Step Guide to Stop Binge Eating; Discover Negative Emotions Behind Your Hunger and Principles of Intuitive Eating to Develop a Healthy Relationship With Food

By
Cristina Collins

Table of Contents

Introduction.. 1

Chapter 1: Emotional Eating -What Is It?......................3

Chapter 2: Principles of Intuitive Eating - An
Overview.. 9

Chapter 3: Food Rules..17

Chapter 4: The Eating Personalities - What Kind of
Eater Are You?.. 21

Chapter 5: Guidelines and Tips to Drop Emotional
Eating Habits.. 33

Chapter 6: Enjoy Food Without Guilt......................... 49

Chapter 7: Body Image.. 57

Chapter 8: Hyperphagia?.. 75

Chapter 9: Food Confusion Leads to Disordered
Eating..84

Chapter 10: Addressing Cravings.................................95

Chapter 11: Natural Detox: What It Is and How to
Speed Up the Process... 102

Chapter 12: The Ultimate Path Toward Healing From Eating Disorders - Knock-Out Tips.............................112

Chapter 13: Eating as Sacred Time: Create the Optimal Eating Environment...120

Chapter 14: Intuitive Eating FAQs..............................129

Chapter 15: Practical Guide to Action........................133

Conclusion...146

Introduction

Diseases are like different dresses: a man puts them on when necessary and takes them off when possible because it rarely happens in life to be naked. It's easier to get sick than to know the truth. Yet the truth exists to those who are willing to seek it. - Anonymous.

Imagine that you quarreled with one of your best friends. Of course, this is temporary, and you will definitely make peace, but now you are upset. You enter the house, and your spouse asks what happened. What will be the answer?

You will honestly tell your husband (or wife), everything and even, perhaps, discuss with him the circumstances and reasons for the quarrel. Say that "all is well," you open the refrigerator in search of ice cream.

But will a box of chocolate ice cream really solve the problem? Or as a result, you just start to feel sickly overeating?

Emotional nutrition is when people use food as a way to

deal with feelings and not to satisfy hunger. We all at least once in our lives ate a packet of cookies from boredom or a box of chocolate in preparation for the exam. But when this happens too often, and especially unconsciously, emotional eating can affect weight, health, and overall well-being.

While not many of us see the connection between food and our senses, understanding what drives emotional eating helps people take steps to break this habit. That is what you should get ready to learn in this book.

Ready?

Chapter 1:

Emotional Eating -What Is It?

Emotional nutrition is one of the methods of short-term relief, which allows you to remove negative emotions through excessive consumption of sweets and fatty foods. This is not a normal response to physical hunger; rather, an impulsive reaction that causes a vicious cycle of overeating, instant gratification of guilt, shame, insecurity. Gradually, you lose control of your feelings, habits, and weight of your body. Then it's time to take action against your worst enemy!

In emotional eaters (people who tend to cope with their emotions with food), attacks of uncontrolled overeating often occur amid anxiety. For example, a difficult exam is ahead, or an important interview, or a trip to the doctor, during which unpleasant health information can be found out, or we do not have time to submit areport in time.

Anxiety is an energy reaction of the body. Receiving an alarm from the brain, the body quickly organizes an energy surge, suggesting that now it will be necessary to run or fight. Therefore, an attack of anxiety is accompanied by motor anxiety, restlessness, a state that people describe with the words "I can't find a place for myself." The real situation at this moment may not require heavy traffic; on the contrary, it may be necessary to calm down and concentrate.

Controlling anxiety takes a lot of resources, and eating is essentially a way to deal with anxiety by responding to emotions. Responding is the reduction of emotion by translating it into active action (running into the kitchen, opening the refrigerator and chewing, chewing, chewing, is also an action!)

Those who have experienced a seizure attack know how difficult it is to stop it simply by volitional effort.

Attempts to "just relax" and "just calm down" also do not work - after half an hour of such relaxation and reassurance, the urge to throw in yourself a kilogram or two calming calories will become completely unbearable.

The connection between mood and food

If you ever found yourself in front of the TV after a hard day, thoughtlessly tasting a spoon of ice cream from a container, you know that mood and food are sometimes connected. The concept of stress nutrition is a proven phenomenon, but at the same time, the relationship between food and real mood disorders, such as depression, also clear. The final association of the diet with the risk of depression has been proven.

In addition to emotional eating, modifiable lifestyle factors, such as dietary choices, smoking, and physical activity, can potentially affect the risk of depression, and work together.
Because we live in a food-rich environment, emotional overeating is an important predictor of obesity and overweight. In a 2006 study of a sample of 1300 respondents, it was demonstrated that for high- emotional eaters, there is a positive relationship between overeating and being overweight. For non-

emotional eaters, such a relationship was not found. These results were confirmed in a long-term study in the study: emotional overeating is enough to cause excess weight.

Basically, emotional overeating precedes weight changes in combination with stress, that is, in connection with stressful life events. In search of the causes of excess weight, it is useful to analyze those stressful events that happened to you several years ago that were enough to change your mood and get a "chain reaction" started.

Impulsive eating and emotional eating

There mostly remains to meet a huge challenge for most people: how to solve the issue of impulsivity that is defined by the fact that an emotion reflexively causes a desire to eat (Emotion -> Want to eat -> Eat). As Pavlov's dog is conditioned to want to eat when he hears the bell, our "patients" are conditioned to want to eat when they hear the sound of emotion. This is the concept of impulsive eating. It, in more ways than one, is intertwined with emotions, and emotional eating.

This mechanism, a consequence of an operant conditioning, results from a negative reinforcement: the ingestion of a rich food manages to relieve momentarily a state of emotional tension. The ingestion behavior thus reinforced, the person develops a behavioral dependence on the food. The more the patient asks for this mechanism, the more the addiction is accentuated, and the more the food response occurs for even low- intensity emotions. The mechanism is aggravated by the fact that the food response itself induces negative emotions related to loss of control and weight gain. Because of the impulsive process, these negative emotions accentuate the desire to eat. The person is trapped in a vicious circle that increases emotional intolerance and can no longer cope with emotional discomfort.

Faced with this vicious circle, the most spontaneous reaction is to reduce the emotional triggers or to try to fight against the urges to eat. In both cases, we engage in an often vain struggle, of which we rarely win.

However, it is possible to consider another alternative that would increase your tolerance to emotional discomfort. To train your inner "him" to better support his emotions, to teach him to observe them, especially by food. Mindfulness leads us to observe and welcome our emotions. This technique teaches us to detect the physical sensations and unpleasant thoughts that accompany them, to observe them with a detached curiosity and without judgment.

This is a tool that could be very powerful, but still needs to be deepened. Hence, I shall start to dig into if from the following chapter.

Chapter 2:
Principles of Intuitive Eating - An Overview

The practice of intuitive nutrition is more than about losing weight. This is about learning how to hear your body. Although for many people, the motivation is related to losing weight.

Nevertheless, the basic principle of intuitive eating - to listen to your body and trust it - remains relevant to all. Developing bodily sensitivity and bodily awareness helps both to relieve emotions and to attain optimal weight.

Intuitive nutrition is not dieting (there are no restrictions on food and mealtime); is not permissiveness (the absence of restrictions does not mean chaos, you just learn to use other ways of regulating nutrition instead of prohibitions); is not a wonderful way that promises you to lose weight in a couple of weeks (a stable good shape is not a miracle, but the result of harmonious relationships with food, which are easy and pleasant to maintain for a long time).

Intuitive nutrition and its 10 principles

1.) Refusal of diets - Diets do not work - everyone knows this, but they continue to starve themselves. They are harmful and useless; after them, you gain weight again. For an intuitive eater, we forget that restrictions generally exist and live without diets!

2.) Eat only when hungry - The wording is hunger is not entirely correct. It is important that you need to eat not only when you begin to feel hunger, but also to stop when the feeling of hunger disappears. Not when you feel full (it comes later), but when hunger is gone! This is difficult, but it is because of this principle that I will answer the question, "is it possible to lose weight on intuitive nutrition" with 100% certainty - yes!

3.) You can eat everything! - Yes, you heard right, there are no more prohibitions! You can eat anything you want at any time of the day. This is the most difficult thing - to afford such a luxury, I know for myself, I need to try to cross the psychological barrier in the head. Pizza in the evening, chocolate before bedtime - everything is possible if you follow the previous point - eat only when you are hungry. This is an intuitive "diet"! At first, you will always want harmful foods, but it will pass very quickly, that's for sure!

4.) Only physical hunger is real - Learn to differentiate physical and emotional hunger. How to recognize hunger? In fact, it is incredibly simple. Physical hunger is felt "by clicking" somewhere in the lower part of the ribs. I know that there are people who, without exaggeration, have not felt physical hunger for years, and this is scary! Do not be afraid to stop eating for the whole day, or maybe for half a day, so that your body finally digests what you put in it and rests. Believe me, when he needs nutrients again, you will definitely understand this!

5.) Counting calories are not important - It is on this diet that counting calories are not important. You still lose your excess weight. We use healthy nutrition for weight loss, and health should be primarily in the head.

6.) Conscious nutrition - Eat beautifully and consciously, enjoy every piece of food that enters your mouth. Beautifully set the table, think about food during the meal, fully focus on this process, without being distracted by any movie or book, and your food will become 100 times tastier. By the way, hunger makes it another million times tastier, so the combination of hunger and awareness is "double kill." You will understand what the real pleasure of eating is!

7.) Food is not a reward - Do not reward yourself with food. You can't think that, for example, I got a promotion at work, so I can eat a cake. You can eat it anytime. Delicious food is now not a gift, but constancy. You eat to live, not live to eat. When you start practicing this point, you'll understand even better how to get rid of overeating, because there will be no more desire to eat all the goodies of the world at a time.

8.) Hobbies and favorite business - Find your favorite pastime, and you will forget about food until you feel real hunger. Do not eat when bored or watching TV shows / in front of the TV. Too many people overeat when they have nothing to do. Find something you'll enjoy more than eating: singing, playing the guitar, drawing, rollerblading, reading books about intuitive eating, for example. Look for yourself!

9.) Fullness in food - Give the body everything it needs. If you are hungry, sitting on proteins and vegetables for weight loss will not work. The body needs carbohydrates and fats, without them you will lose health, and ultimately a beautiful figure, when you start to gobble up (and you will start if you only eat what does not bring energy).

10.) Self-love - Accept and respect your body now, you will have no other. When you start lovingly and gratefully treating your "vessel," the shell that allows you to exist. In this world, you will no longer want to litter it with excess food and begin to nourish it with good, healthy, wholesome food. Therefore, we are talking about intuitive nutrition! Nutrition of the body! Our biological membrane serves and tries for us every day. She is ready to work 100% unless you poison her. Our consciousness cannot exist without a body. We depend on it; we must love it because it is the main thing that allows us to live on our planet!

Benefits of intuitive eating

These feedback and principles will help you to establish psychological and physical harmony, followed by weight loss if everything is done correctly. When you put your thoughts in order, your nutrition will improve - forced dieting will no longer be needed.

The other advantage of intuitive nutrition, of course, is the absence of any framework, whether it be time limits or the use of any products. When used correctly, the system of intuitive nutrition is absolutely harmless to the body. You are allowed to eat all products, regardless of their protein, fat, or carbohydrate content. You can do whatever you want at any time. The main thing to observe the principles is when you are hungry and not eat if you are full.

With sufficient physical activity, after a month, you will notice that the weight is leaving. The quality of life improves, positive emotions are added.

Why diets don't work and why it's not about the food

The body exists according to a clearly planned algorithm by nature. The heart, kidneys, stomach, and other organs work like clockwork, unless, of course, they are destroyed. Fat is also part of a well-functioning system that lends itself to very specific patterns. One of them: if the number of incoming calories decreases sharply, the body turns on the emergency mode of self-defense.

First, the hormones responsible for appetite get out of hand. When we starve, a part of the brain called the hypothalamus triggers a defense mechanism. As a result, we become gluttonous and unable to control ourselves by willpower. So nighttime glitches and breakdowns are a physiological mechanism by which the body protects itself.

Secondly, the loss of kilograms on diets occurs due to dehydration and a decrease in muscle tissue. Fat is the last to suffer. Not only that, the body begins to produce even less fat-releasing and fat-burning enzymes, such as hormone-sensitive lipase and lipoprotein lipase. Fat- burning hormones are destroyed, including T3, the active form of the thyroid hormone, which plays an important role in the regulation of metabolism.

Thirdly, after the end of the diet, the weight returns with an increase. This is primarily due to a slowdown in metabolism. During the diet, the body devours its own muscle tissue. So even when you return to your usual diet after a low-calorie unbalanced diet, we gain fat.

Fourth, after a tough diet, we start to ... sorry, eat. In scientific language, this is called compensatory overeating. So the body prepares for a possible repetition of a hunger strike - it stores as much fat as possible and spends it less and less willingly.

The body is cunning; it quickly adapts, reducing the level of metabolism and thereby reducing calorie consumption. After all, the metabolism does not care that you want to look beautiful in a swimsuit. He perceives the diet as a threat of starvation and reduces the metabolic rate in order to save our lives.

Chapter 3:
Food Rules

According to studies, 95% of people who follow strict diets gain even more weight within 5 years. Diets are an example of imitation and self-imposed persecution in modern society. In fact, they put great stress on the body, and this is not good. Hence the need to examine your food rules.

Examine your food rules

With proper nutrition, the mealtime should be accurately compensated, since only the timely intake of nutrients can compensate for energy costs. For a healthy person, the most rational is a four-time diet. With it, a uniform load on the digestive system is provided; food is better digested and absorbed.

With two meals a day, with intervals between meals up to 7 hours or more, the level of cholesterol in the blood increases, fat deposits accumulate, the intensity of the thyroid gland decreases. In addition, after a long interval, a person can immediately eat a lot of food, overflowing the stomach and reducing the mobility of its walls. Stretching the stomach not only negatively affects the quality of digestion of food, but also raises the diaphragm, interfering with normal cardiac activity.

Long breaks cause the release of a large volume of gastric juice and irritation of the gastric mucosa. Too small breaks between meals are also undesirable. Time for the complete digestion process, in this case, is not enough, which can lead to an upset digestive tract. A very important factor in the organization of a healthy diet is the regularity of food intake.

By a certain time, a person has a feeling of hunger, which triggers the secretion of gastric juice, necessary for digesting food. With violations of the diet, this reflex in a person fades. Food enters the stomach, which is not yet ready for the digestion process. As a result, appetite decreases, and all the food that enters the body is very poorly absorbed, which causes gastritis, cholecystitis, and other diseases. As practice shows, listening to your body and satisfying it in a timely manner is the best bet.

Your family's food rules
Intuitive eating is not only healthy but also delicious. In addition, the products in your dishes contain all the right

nutrients down to the necessary set of vitamins and minerals.

How to instill healthy eating habits in your family's diet? According to experts, any habit can be formed in 21 days. The same statement applies to healthy eating. These habits are not at all difficult to instill; you only need to set a clear goal and not step back from it.

Take note of a few helpful tips:

Ask yourself - why do I want to change my eating habits? The answer should be as specific as possible, and the ultimate goal achievable. For example, lose weight by three kilograms, improve complexion, get rid of heartburn, etc.

Avoid hard limits - Do not force yourself not to eat after 18.00, to completely any type of food. All these prohibitions lead to stress and the abandonment of attempts to change habits for the better. Before eating habits have not changed, feel free to take your family to cafes and restaurants, forgetting that there are too many temptations. Over time, a natural preference will set in for homemade food.

Do not pay attention to attacks from the outside - just learn how to find decent answers to comments about your new food preferences. This is especially true for joint tea parties with sweets and cookies.

In fact, changing your eating habits is not that difficult. Together with regular sports, smoking cessation, and a positive outlook, it becomes a new lifestyle for the family.

Chapter 4:
The Eating Personalities - What Kind of Eater Are You?

According to a Swiss study, our personality traits dictate our food choices. If some represent risk factors, taking them into account would help us find a healthy lifestyle.

However, across all personality traits, the data collected suggests that a lack of self-discipline causes some people to eat impulsively and not be able to control themselves in front of food that smells good.

While neurotic people tend to choose caloric foods to cope with their negative emotions, extroverts would be more likely to adopt poor eating habits because of external factors such as smell or taste of food. Their high level of sociability leads them to have more meals in company.

The good news is that taking into account our personality traits would help regulate our bad habits and restore a balanced lifestyle.

Chaotic unconscious eater

This group represents 18% of the population; it is composed mostly of women (70%) rather young - two- thirds are under fifty. Caloric intake is low, but their dietary diversity is limited. Chaotic unconscious eaters are the strongest consumers of pastries, pizzas, and quiches, but the frequency of overweight and obesity is low. This group has a high risk of deficiency, folate deficiency, calcium, vitamin C, magnesium, and fiber remaining low.

Nutritional advice:

- Restore diversity to prevent deficiencies.

The careful eater

This group represents 27% of the population, with a majority of women and two-thirds over the age of forty- five. It is characterized by the absence of food preferences and a level of consumption of all food categories close to the average. While this remains true, the careful eater is mostly obsessed with the components in the food. Overweight is common in this group.

Nutritional advice:

- Maintain food diversification, while following a less "bookish" recommendations to achieve a balanced diet: a little more fruits and vegetables and a little less caloric foods, for example.

- Increase physical activity.

The unconscious eater

This group represents 14% of the population, with a slight majority of men and three-quarters of people between eighteen and thirty-four. Unconscious eaters are the strongest consumers of sweet biscuits, rice, pasta, soda, and chocolate. The low frequency of obesity in this group is explained by the average age, which is quite low. The problem is to know to which consumer profile these young eaters will evolve into with age.

Nutritional advice:

- Diversify the diet, eat more fruits and vegetables and fewer sweets.

- Prevent the risk of obesity by restoring good eating habits, fighting sedentariness, and promoting physical activity.

Evaluate your belief system about food and your body

As you might already know, if we take the time to question our behavior, they can tell a lot about certain traits of our temperament and how we work with eating habits. Self-observation with attention and especially with kindness helps to decode and/or better understand sometimes unexplored facets of ourselves, and this is also the whole purpose of emotional eating therapy.

To shorten it,

- those who like thrills, take risks or aspire to be the focus of attention would be attracted to spicy food;

- sweet beaks and other sweet food lovers would be people with pro-social functions, i.e., friendly, helpful, caring and caring people;

- bitter food lovers could be synonymous with a narcissistic, Machiavellian, and even psychopathic nature. Beware to lovers of coffee, chicory, or dark chocolate!

Obviously, presented like this, the reasoning seems simplistic! It is, however, more or less the results advanced by the researchers in neurology and psychology at the initiative of these studies which proceed on the principle that:

- all our behaviors reflect in a certain way our personality (in which it is difficult not to agree);

- but our tastes and food preferences have developed at the same time as the personality (that is to say over the period from 0 to 7 years),

- and the places responsible for our personality and the olfactory and taste systems are anatomically close in the brain.

I am not a specialist, but I admit that correlating the tastes and personality of an individual on the basis of these criteria is a concern. Because in my humble opinion, the reality is much more complex! Already because the food is also social (and not only identity).

The differences in tastes from one individual to another are not only to be found in taste receptors (thus on a genetic level), they are also closely related to social and cultural factors.

Our tastes express our belonging to groups and are largely influenced by our origins and our culture, sometimes without our knowledge. It is enough to observe eating habits in adolescence to find that eating is also expressing one's style or that of the peer group one has chosen. And this obviously persists in adulthood! Our food tastes speak volumes about who we are and the groups we belong to. The taste is even, first of all, a proof of knowledge: we talk about good taste and "make the palate" as an apprenticeship, or even a badge belonging to the upper classes!

How to evaluate your beliefs and eat the right foods intuitively?

Of course, there are also some universal tastes or almost! Just about everyone likes chocolate so much that those who are not fond of it are regarded as aliens. We all have an innate fondness for the sweet, which makes this flavor one of our main sources of pleasure and comfort throughout life. But taste remains above all the fruit of learning and is, therefore, part of the intuitive eating guide. It is a construction that is set up following early and repeated experiences. It is by testing various tastes from an early age that preferences develop and evolve, sharpen, become more specific, and I have trouble believing that the personality has something to do with it.

A multitude of external factors plays on the taste, among which:

- archaic criteria: studies have revealed that it is mainly color that guides us in our food choices: red food is perceived as much richer in calories than green foods, we are naturally and instinctively attracted by this type of food.

- unconscious criteria: sight influences taste, especially through the mechanism of food inferences, namely that the appearance of a product will infer its presumed taste. To save time, it's as if our brain was associating ideas. It is from this observation that neurogastronomy develops and tries to introduce auditory, visual, olfactory, tactile elements to influence the perception of flavors.

- our appetites for this or that food are also influenced by the context of tasting: the presence of other guests pushes us to eat like them to join the group; the fact that there is a choice at the table opens the appetite, and we consume about 17% more. Even the weather has an impact on our taste! That the one who does not tend to eat more and/or to be attracted by more invigorating dishes may eat more when it is cold!

Finally, emotion plays a role in our appetence for this or that food.

So, must we subscribe in full to the famous aphorism "I eat so I am"? The answer? Yes! This allows us to wonder and explore facets of our personality and annihilate the desire to find answers based on emotions or popular belief!

Self-acceptance

Self-acceptance is defined as "the acceptance of all your attributes, positive or negative." You understand and accept your body's acceptance, and offer yourself self- protection from negative critics.

Poor self-acceptance can disrupt emotional control in two ways: directly, by disrupting the areas of the brain that control it, and indirectly by increasing stress signals in your brain that then disrupt those areas. These factors only push you much farther into the emotional eating trail.

Ways to increase self-acceptance

1.) Self-regulation - This involves taking distance from negative emotions such as self-rejection, and refocusing on the positive aspects of yourself, or reframing negative situations so that you see them more as opportunities. Good knowledge of oneself also makes it easier to accept one's own limits. When you transcend, physical changes occur in your brain, such as the increase of the neurotransmitter serotonin, in the same brain regions that are affected by self-acceptance.

2.) Meditation as a path to self-acceptance - Self- acceptance can develop through two types of meditation: mindfulness meditation and benevolent love meditation. Conscious attention to one's emotions means not to "judge" them, but to observe them as they present themselves. Having more compassion for yourself seems useful for increasing self-acceptance. The most important thing is to find the right ways that work for you. It's worth it because self-acceptance is one of the keys to a healthy emotional and psychological life!

Developing a supportive inner voice

Listening to one's inner voice, one's subconsciousness, or trusting one's intuition allows one to make better decisions, seize new opportunities, dare to step out of one's comfort zone, and even avoid embarrassing situations. This is an important element to consider if you want fewer emotional moments in your life. A supportive inner voice is a great ally for the first time facing a new situation. To know how to listen to it, however, is not always obvious. Some work is needed on this aspect, especially when you have to make choices under pressure. Here are five tips that will help you.

Ways to develop a supportive inner voice

1.) Spend time with people who do not belong to your professional circle - Indulge in an activity that is not related to any tough decision to be made. This is an opportunity to take a step back and dilute the importance of the problem, especially when it is complex.

2.) Be emphatic - Emphasize and value your environment, your own emotions, and those of others. In other words, be emphatic. You will bring out the positive. This is excellent if you are in the process of analyzing the "for" and "against" of a problem.

3.) Cultivate moments of loneliness - By giving yourself moments of relaxation, you are attracting opportunities to be alone with yourself. You must breathe and be attentive to your body. In my case, when I have to make important choices, I am more attentive to the physical reactions felt when I am calm. I also become more considerate.

4.) Accumulate information - Do you feed information? The more you consult and document, the more you will recognize your limits to move forward. For my part, I have this need to feel that I went around different solutions before making a decision. By learning as much as possible, I feel certain security when I hear my little inner voice give me a line of thought.

5.) Chasing the negative - Finally, see the positive behind the negative of a situation. If not, your inner voice can become an obstacle to achieving your goals. It may send you the message that your goals are not achievable. It reflects your own thoughts or feelings. I realized that when my inner voice acted this way, it was because I did not have enough confidence in my abilities. I know today that I can manage it better. After all, "she" does not have absolute control of my life.

Now you have the floor. Do you ever listen to your inner voice?

Chapter 5:
Guidelines and Tips to Drop
Emotional Eating Habits

Honor your hunger

Respect your hunger and do not divide products into strictly useful and strictly harmful. If your hunger is really physical and your body suddenly requires one and a half times more food than usual, analyze the past day: if you spent half a day in the gym, cleaning or in exhausting shopping, it is possible that your body needs exactly this amount of food to restore strength.

The same story with conditionally harmful and conditionally useful products: If the body does not want another vegetable soup, but requires a piece of cake, reconsider your diet. Perhaps your food is completely varied, and you should include nuts, avocados, legumes, fruits, and meat. If everything is in order, but the body continues to demand a burger from McDonald's, go and eat it: so you will avoid a breakdown, and you will not find yourself a week later, roaring at an empty box of burgers.

Make peace with food

Do not forget about aesthetics. Intuitive nutrition is, in many ways, about love. Love for your body, appearance, body, and food. That is why it is better to have lunch in a comfortable and pleasant environment. A pizza slice and a light salad that you slowly eat in your favorite Italian cafe will not do you much more harm than "healthy" carrot sticks swallowed on the run.

Feel your fullness

Respect the feeling of fullness and remember the beauty and health of your body. Yes, there really is everything, but in reasonable quantities. It's best to use the French rule: sometimes at dinner they can afford an extra glass of champagne and a slice of baguette with foie gras, but at the same time, they are fully aware that this guilty pleasure should not be allowed daily, but for a serving of dishes when full it would be nicer to swim a pool instead.

Discover the satisfaction factor

Perhaps the highest skill in intuitive nutrition is to find your point of satisfaction (satiety). The inhabitants of Asian countries have always succeeded in this. There are practically no obese people in the east, although they have always believed that food is one of the greatest pleasures. They only eat when they are hungry. And they stop clearly when they are full. Follow these rules, and you should eat slowly, consciously, savoring every bite. There is nothing wrong with enjoying a meal. Only now you need to enjoy the quality of food, not its quantity.

Cope with your emotions without using food

All negative conditions (anger, boredom, anger, resentment, anxiety, despondency) must be learned to be sorted out as independent issues, not with food. Look for ways to calm yourself without food, because it will not solve your problems.

Respect your body

Accept yourself as you are. Respect what nature has given you. Accept your genetics and do not demand the impossible from your body. Paradoxically, only by accepting and loving your body unconditionally, you will want to improve it. But within reasonable limits and without undue violence.

Address needs and set nurturing limits

Although several reasons may explain the ingrained habit of eating too much, the most spontaneous and common answer is always "it's good, eat". Behind this affirmation, there is this pleasure associated with the natural instinct of survival which is in us and which dictates to us to eat when the food is accessible.

Nowadays, the great pleasure of eating is that it can be done effortlessly because many foods are already ready to eat without having to cook them. The challenge set nurturing limits for eating by programming; otherwise, our survival instinct that is always present because it is an integral part of human nature.

How to getting started

Solutions?

In private consultation, I use a tool that allows the person to ask themselves a series of questions before eating, to assess whether it is justifiable and relevant to do so at this time. Here are the questions:

In your opinion, do the food industry and advertising push you to eat too much? Do you think that stress and low self-esteem lead to your overeating? Are you attracted to sugary, fatty, and salty foods? Are they for you a form of reward? What strategies have you developed to resist these foods?

By dint of asking these different questions, I think it is possible to come to plan to eat only for the physiological needs of hunger rather than being a puppet that is manipulated by his emotions, in addition, to undergo the influence of incentive ads, people around you, opportunities of all kinds, variable meal times, etc. I also agree with those who advocate regulation to ban or at least reduce advertising incentives for junk food.

I think we eat too much because our diet is often unbalanced and includes foods that are not complete enough and nutritious. A sandwich of white bread and ham with fruit juice and some biscuits cannot give us much energy and support us for a long time.

The last bite threshold - Step-by-step guidelines to addressing needs and setting nurturing limits

1.) Drink a glass of water: why not? It's zero calories. We hydrate ourselves. Only positive.

2.) We go out of the kitchen: Far from visual temptations, far from the fridge and closet, we are less tempted!

3.) We will brush our teeth: Yes, you read that, we will wash our teeth no matter what time it is. It is a very powerful technique that will allow several things:

- to have a fresh taste in the mouth

- take no pleasure in the 1st bite straight up after brushing

- to really make the difference between the desire to nibble and the real feeling of hunger that pulls the stomach, and that will not disappear while brushing the teeth!

4.) Going for a walk (or running, or cycling, or swimming, or jumping rope, or dancing, or doing yoga, or going to a garden): In short, you will understand, moving is a good opportunity to pleasantly to avoid nibbling. I insist on the "pleasantly." It's important to choose something that you like — no way to ride a bike if you hate it. The "no pain, no gain" (it is necessary to suffer to have result) is old-fashioned! Opt for 100% pleasure but no side effect, unlike nibbling, that has a negative effect.

5.) Play music (or play an instrument): This can be called music therapy. It takes away your tensions of the day and your black ideas! For me, I know that they are very specific songs with, e.g., trumpet or African style music that makes me go back to the wave. I feel like my cells line up when I listen to this!

6.) Read a book: It allows us to disconnect by diving into another universe. Okay, right now, I'm reading a book where the heroine is holding a cupcake. While this may not be the best example of a book to advise you to avoid nibbling… good … just choose another!

7.) Take care of yourself in the bathroom: simply a hot shower, a relaxing bath, wax or shave, making a facial, etc. I insist, at any time of the day! It works, do it!

In fact, we can find much more than 7 things to do to avoid nibbling; I could extend the list with:

- make a phone call to a friend,

- search for information on the internet for various projects in progress (a trip, new decor for the room, etc.),

- watch an episode of your favorite series (except if being passive in front of a screen makes you want to nibble),

I'm joking a bit, but for some people, the food compulsion (or overeating, that is to say eating a lot without having control) is anchored, and it is difficult to dislodge, despite all the goodwill we put in it. One of the solutions is to break this nibbling routine by planning "fun actions" at crucial moments in the day it happens. Attention, we do not break a bad habit by eating fruit. No, if you're not hungry, it's important to do something other than eating!

For example, plan that when you come home from work, you will:

- Monday, walk

- Tuesday, take a bath

- Wednesday, book your holidays on the internet

- Thursday, read a book

- Friday, call a friend.

In fact, nibbling habits are of interest; they serve to reduce tensions, for example. But using food to solve your psychological difficulties is not the right solution. On the other hand, I know it's very, very easy to eat when you're not hungry.

Yes, food can be a refuge, it soothes us, and we sometimes use it to fight stress, boredom, or oppressive emotional states. The good news is that we are able to regulate our food intake. By nature, the body is well done, and it's up to him to ask! Yes, the secret is to know how to listen to him and trust him: to give him food when he asks (hunger), and not to give him when he does not ask. It requires to be extremely attentive, I agree, at least at the beginning we practice, then it becomes natural.

Taking additional practical steps

You are not alone in thinking that all the efforts you make during the week are wiped out by your weekend excesses. I am often asked how to be more "reasonable" when it comes to the weekend. My answer is surely not the one you think.

1.) We must get rid of our "rules" food

Food rules are rules that are imposed and dictate what to eat or not to eat, when to eat or not to eat, how to eat, how much to eat, etc. I give you an example: I do not drink wine from Monday to Thursday. I only drink it on the weekends.

These rules are often very restrictive and not realistic. They are too difficult to follow, and eventually, you will certainly break them. What is happening at that time? Not only do we feel guilty of breaking a rule, but we also think that our entire weekend is fucked up, and we get into the all-or-nothing mentality, which brings me to my next point.

2.) We must get rid of the mentality of all or nothing.
We want to do everything to eat well. We follow a strict food plan, our portions are controlled, and we avoid eating some of our favorite foods since they are supposedly fattening. All week, we are worried about making a mistake. Arrive at the weekend, and we cannot stop eating the same thing, the cravings are becoming stronger and "lack of will" we let go. It's landed. And what a landfall!

We must not aim for perfection, but rather for progress. We must adopt food behaviors that are sustainable. For example, I really want to eat pasta tonight. The last time I ate it, I abused it a bit and got a stomach ache later. I will start with a small portion, take the time to savor each bite, and I will stop to eat when I'm no longer hungry. Or again: I really want a hamburger, but the fries on the side, I do not care so much, and I'll opt for a salad instead. Regardless of your food choice, make sure you feel comfortable with this decision, both while eating and afterward. A more moderate approach that is sustainable is worth much more than a "perfect" approach that cannot be followed for more than a few days.

3.) We must get rid of the famous "cheat day." For those who are not familiar with the cheat day, this is a day in the week when "everything is allowed" and without limit. This is a way that many use to reward themselves for having had their diet during the previous 6 days. Then comes the food orgy - we finally eat all the food we have defended all week. The cheat day is over, and knowing that the next day is the return to reality, we start to worry (and maybe to eat more). It is the return to purgatory for 6 days. It is not a very beautiful relation with the food which one builds at this time. The solution is to get rid of the cheat day and give yourself permission to choose what you want all week, not just the weekend.

4.) We must stop rationalizing our food choices. The weekend seems to set us traps and pushes us to eat more. The reasons are multiple. We're on the road, we have a family meal, we're busy, it's someone's party, we're alone at home, and we have nothing to do. Allthe excuses are good.

Traveling, being busy, or family dinners do not cause overconsumption. We eat and drink too much in all kinds of situations. The reason we give ourselves for eating too much is simply consistent with what is happening at that time.

Rationalizing our eating behavior in this way invites us to believe that we cannot do anything about it, and also pushes us to repeat this behavior.

It's time to ask the real questions: why am I eating too much in such a situation? Am I stressed, sad, or happy? Does food become a loophole? Do I impose too many restrictions on the week? Has food become one of my only pleasures? Or the only way to reward me? We must dare to ask these questions to find the solution.

If you have recognized yourself a few times in the behaviors described above, a healthier look at your body discussed earlier would help you regain balance and solidify a healthy relationship with food.

Name and track emotions and bodily sensations Newborns, we knew how to eat intuitively: we askedfor food when we were hungry and stopped suckling when we were no longer hungry.

What happened next?

The cultural and educational messages have diverted from us intuitive messages of our body and replaced them with: "finished the food on your plate," "eat otherwise you will be hungry," "must not spoil"... Then, society insidiously distilled the messages of thinness and diet - sometimes from childhood. Then, the abundant societies in which we live have also made immediate and infinite food available.

Intuitive eating allows you to re-learn the "intuitive eating" that we have lost. Thus, eating intuitively allows you to re-eat in a flexible way, tracking emotions and body sensations, being attentive to your food sensations of hunger and satiety to know when to eat, what to eat and when to stop eating. Intuitive eating gives you confidence in your body, who knows better thananyone what it needs.

The underlying principle is listening to the body: this ability to be in contact with what is happening in one's body, then to nourish the needs of the body by taking care of oneself and engaging in the process of kindness towards it.

Practice self- validation

You have already experienced this great moment of loneliness tinged with emotional upheaval totally disordered before a piece of cake that makes you an eye. It is said that eating is a matter of common sense, but in the end, you agree? Eating is not so easy. Because this piece of cake, it is so associated with all sorts of emotions and questions, not counting the eyes of others, that finally, we do not even know if we are hungry, or if we just want to eat it. If we deprive ourselves or if we abstain. Well, precisely, the intuitive diet is there to help us find the natural instinct of eating.

The idea here is not to lose weight but to find a feeling of peace with oneself, with one's body, with food, and with all the emotions associated with it. No one and no external emotions, not even yours, should affect your eating choice. If you are hungry and you have a craving for food, it is yours for the taking!

Reinforce self-validation

In fact, you'll just have to do one thing, one little thing: trust yourself. Do you want to eat? Eat! Do you prefer a chocolate custard rather than an apple for dessert? Go for it! Do you want chocolate right away? Jump at the chocolate! In fact, you have to imagine that you are a little child who does not yet pose all these poisonous questions like "I should," "I should not," "and my pounds!" Or, a classic, "I'm not allowed to eat yet even though I'm hungry, it's not time!" And finally, make it clear as water that pours forth from a rock: become again this child who eats according to his needs.

Using all your senses to explore, savor, and taste Children develop their taste and discover foods using their five senses. As you enjoy a glass of good wine, fine chocolate, or a new cheese flavor, remember that eating is a multisensory experience! Help yourself return to childhood and become fully aware of each of your senses and appreciate it in relation to the food(s) on your plate.

Chapter 6:
Enjoy Food Without Guilt

Yes, you can learn this - relish food with a light heart without being nervous, although constant talk about the malignity of fat and sweet does not contribute to this. Food psychotherapists explain how our prejudices prevent us from enjoying peacefully.

"She slowly brings to her lips a spoonful of chocolate mousse, which she so wanted, and not a drop of guilt will not spoil this moment of pure pleasure. For her, this chocolate is not a problem; it does not threaten either her figure or her peace of mind. She has no thoughts in her mind that she is doing something bad because she does not consider chocolate a forbidden product. She will not punish herself by eating kefir alone, but she also does not want to take a second dessert."

If you, reading these lines, sighed with envy ("I would like to be in her place!") Or fell into a gloom ("I can never do this ..."), these savoring lessons are created just for you. Especially if you quench your gourmet outbursts or, conversely, do not know the measures in food, while experiencing an acute sense of guilt. "If gluttony, one of the seven deadly sins, which in our culture still enjoys a bad reputation, it is because it has taken on the whole burden of Puritan morality and prejudice, the object of which was previously sexuality" food psychotherapists analyze.

I have selected the six most common statements and opinions reflecting our inability to combine food joys and peace of mind. Having familiarized yourself with the advice of food psychotherapists, you will understand what prevents you from fully surrendering to your desire to eat delicious food, and you will be able to learn a different attitude to foods and dishes that you still considered dangerous.

1.) "I know that I certainly shouldn't, but ..." What is happening in your head :"I should not have" indicates that you are guided by two types of norms in your behavior: on the one hand, moral (I can't break the ban, but I don't have enough willpower), and on the other - the norms of eating behavior (it's fatty, it's sweet, and that's bad). These words, which your inner voice whispers, refer you to the widely spread and supported by various kinds of "food observers by the rules" idea that some products always get people fat, while   others   we   supposedly   can use   in   practically unlimited quantities without any for potential risk factors for ourselves because they have few calories.

The path to change

At the moment, when you are trying to reason yourself and at the same time are ready to give up, ask yourself the questions: "Is my appetite strong enough to appreciate this chocolate? Can I experience real pleasure?" If you answered "yes" to both questions, calmly allow yourself this moment of pleasure. If the answer is no, do something else. In an hour, in the evening or tomorrow, chocolate will be exactly what you need, but not right now. The decision is entirely up to you, so it will not cause you any frustration. This exercise aims to make you face your true needs. They should be the driving force of your choice.

2.) "Better I'll stay away from this."

What is happening in your head: "Where it leads me, I can't resist anymore," you tell yourself. Since you doubt your ability to withstand "hostile" products, it seems more reasonable to exercise your willpower by keeping your distance from them, rather than consuming them calmly and moderately. This behavior reflects a fear of losing control of the situation and, therefore, a fear of one's own desires.

The path to change

You need to tame a tabooed product, stop being afraid of it and give it a proper place. You can practice this way: use only this product for several meals to make sure that by itself it does not lead to fullness. For example, for three days in one of your main meals (preferably at lunch), limit yourself to chocolate; taste it slowly and thoughtfully, stopping at the moment when you feel full. It is important to accurately catch when you are already full and stop before you feel upcoming nausea. You will see that you will not increase kilograms.

3.) "If I do not resist, then I will go on a diet."

What happens in your head: You allow yourself pleasure - provided that it will be followed by punishment! This dialectical approach, seemingly rational and balanced, is actually misleading and generally harmful. It only reinforces the notion that some products are "bad," and others are "good." In fact, it enhances the attraction to illicit foods and the aversion to foods that you punish yourself. A great way to accustom yourself even more to desire chocolate and hate vegetables and greens even more!

The path to change

Give up diets! Trust yourself; just listen to your own appetite. Few people manage to continuously eat heavy and fatty foods without experiencing physical discomfort. Wait calmly until the feeling of hunger returns to you naturally, then allow yourself to follow your desires. If you have a feeling that you have abused a product, do not demonize it because its attractiveness for a while will naturally come to naught. When you want to eat this product again, you will do it with pleasure.

4.) "It and when I start to eat it, then I can't stop." What is happening in your head: This is a good example of the implacable logic of "all or nothing." The desired product is equated with sin: to remain "innocent" and stay away from the temptation or, if we have not resisted, to reach the bottom in its fall. Violation of the ban creates an emergency: you want to immediately and fully take advantage of your "crime," which gives you more pleasure than the absorption of the product itself. The price that you have to pay is high - this, of course, is a feeling of guilt.

The path to change

Describe the object of your desire for a halo of exclusivity. This box of sweets or slices of ham, shining ominously and enticingly, of course, deserve to be eaten more often - then they will finally lose their imaginary power over you. Eat them every time (yes, yes!). Then focus on tasting to catch the point of the highest pleasure. Over time, you will learn to stop at this moment, completely naturally and without any frustration.

5.) "I choose the least-priced high-calorie goodies."

What is happening in your head: You give yourself the pleasure to control your desire by deceiving it! Using only substitutes, you experience not sensual, but intellectual pleasure, namely the joy of owning a situation! In addition, you think that pleasure is in quantity, not quality. But such reasoning leads to bulimia, which we indirectly encourage by promoting the so-called light or dietary products.

The path to change

Develop your taste buds. Discover the taste of real food, and you will realize how tasteless its pale copies are. Why not arrange a short session of comparative tasting and choose between real natural yogurt and its low-fat counterpart? Developing your taste, you will no longer try to drown out frustration due to quantity (a bar of diet chocolate instead of two truffles). Savoring a quality product, you will learn to stop when you are full.

6.) "I break the diet when I feel bad."

What is happening in your head: Food is not a pleasure in itself; for you, it is a form of protection from obscure and poorly controlled emotions. A bag of candies that we absorb, thinking about something else, a hearty dish that we pounce on to calm down ... Unconsciously, you think that suffering gives you the right to allow yourself too much.

The path to change

Recognize your emotions. Nutrition is that shield with which we fence ourselves off from them. If your need for comfort in difficult times is met with certain products, do not add guilt to your suffering. Allow yourself to improve your condition, but then return to what happened. Have you experienced anger, sadness, anxiety, or stress? Identify the emotion that made you fall into emotional despair. Gradually, you will stop drowning out emotions that overwhelm you in this way with food, and you will look them directly in the face. You will become internally more independent and return the food to its proper place: pleasure, not a shield.

Chapter 7:
Body Image

Body image disorders are obviously associated with the desire to lose weight. We do not like our bodies, so we try to control it, to modify it because we were made to believe we could do it. And this has many repercussions on our life: isolation, depression, excessive control ... Is there not another way out of this infernal spiral of dissatisfaction?

Balanced weight vs. ideal weight

The first thing to understand is that the idea that we control our weight is an illusion. Already, your weight is programmed in a genetic way. Then your food and personal stories have meant that your body needs to reach a certain weight (balanced weight) that probably does not fit your ideal body. The more we do the "yoyo," the more we gain weight.

So there is a good chance that the weight you dream of does not match your weight balance. Clearly, if you try to reach a weight lower than your balance weight, your body will do everything to make you find this weight.

That's why (among other things), you regain your weight after a diet.

I repeat again here that diets do not work: in all cases, people regain their weight (in a huge number, they regain more weight). So, understand that you cannot control your weight, or you will have to be on a diet all your life.

The pressures related to the ideal of thinness
Of course, knowing that diets do not work is not enough because we live in a society where we are bombarded with injunctions to modify this body considered imperfect.

Wherever we look, we are asked to make efforts. We are told that our body is not acceptable (whether big orthin for that matter).

And the worst is that like us, our peers, our friends, our family, our colleagues, are affected by these injunctions. Today, we have all come to believe that thinness = happiness. We all ended up believing that fat is bad.

Prejudice and beliefs about obesity are widespread and spread throughout society. Everyone participates in this pressure on the body. Even here in the U.S., our way of looking at our body is to judge it, to compare it, and to do the same with others.

Discrimination against obese people is ubiquitous (e.g., professional, medical). Yet, making people ashamed to encourage them to lose weight is counterproductive and leads to isolation, disconnection from their body, depression, etc.

We begin to recognize the grossophobia infiltrated on all levels of society (and in every corner of our head). Of course, it will take time for society to change, and many of us are actively working on it.

Our representation of the perfect body feeds our body dissatisfaction and our desires to control our body - by the control of our food (most often resulting in bouts of emotional eating), cosmetic surgery, sport, etc.

Faced with the constant solicitations of society, taking a fresh look at the body, caring, can be extremely difficult or almost impossible. But, at your level, there are two or three things you can do to improve your body image anyway. Remember, however, that a good body image does not depend on its weight.

Negative body talk - 5 tips for moving forward on the path of acceptance

1.) Take the distance from the images that are conveyed in the media
Yes, we are shown perfect women, but no, these women do not really exist. You can choose to detoxify groups, pages, blogs that promote thinness, the cult of the ideal body, slimming recipes, sports to lose weight. Stop. We've had enough!

2.) As you cannot change your entire environment, you will still be affected by these images. And even if these images hurt you, what makes you even more so, is to believe them, and to **cultivate in you a disenchantment.**

Of course, you will always have thoughts of the style "you are too fat," you are ugly" etc. But ask yourself:

- How are these thoughts useful to me?
- How do I feel these thoughts?
- Do they lead me to live the life I want?

And if it's not the case, if these thoughts weaken you and make you hate you more and more, do not listen to them anymore. Take distance. Your thoughts are just words, and like these photoshopped images, they often do not tell the truth. Detoxify your thoughts!

3.) Take a caring attitude towards your body
Maybe, in the beginning, it will be artificial, but over time, you will learn to be gentler with yourself. Take care of yourself. Treat yourself with respect:

-Reconnect with your body. Take the time to listen to yourself (mindfulness meditation, breaks, time for yourself, physical activity).

-Reconnect positive sensations with your body:

a) Observe your body. Take the time, if possible, every day, to observe yourself in the mirror. Become aware of the judgments that will emerge spontaneously and try to look beyond. You have heard these judgments millions of times, but who are you?

Remember that these are harmful thoughts that do not move you forward. If you are overweight, you are also more than an overweight person. Your body is more than a big belly. Observe it in its entirety.

b) Take the time to touch your body, to appreciate its contours, the quality of your skin, the sensations brought by this touch. You can massage by starting with a body part, perhaps a neutral part like the hands. Then gradually, attack the parties that are problematic. These parts of your body are part of you and deserve your attention (even if you do not like them).

4.) Take care of yourself

You do not have to wait for a body that satisfies you to take care of you. Certainly, you have learned to be ashamed of your body, because considered "unsuitable," but all this is false. You have the right to respect and your body too. So you have a duty to take care of yourself today! That is to say, to do things that give you energy and make you happy.

- What activities give you energy?
- What activities give you pleasure?
- What would you like to do for you?

Are there things you do not do because of your bodily concerns? I invite you to do one or more of these things. This should increase your self-confidence and contradict your fears. Yes, you can go to the pool. Yes, you can do yoga.

5.) Develop a caring voice

You probably tend to denigrate all day long; to always demand more of yourself, never to be satisfied: this is called perfectionism. Perfectionism is rigidity. The opposite of what we are looking for to live a fulfilling life.

To stop looking for perfection is not to let go. It is accepting what cannot be changed and doing what it takes to change what is in our power.

You will never reach a state where you will be perfect, where you will no longer need to evolve, where you will be sufficient. You will always be imperfect, and will always make mistakes. It is the characteristic of humans.

To help you fight against your perfectionism, which pushes you to adopt rigid rules for supposedly becoming "better," you must work to develop that caring voice that cares for you.

This benevolent voice is the observer in you, who is able to see in a neutral way freed from automatic thoughts gathered from your different experiences. This caring voice can help you make choices that will lead you to a better life (rather than automatically repeating harmful behaviors).

To develop this voice, you must become accustomed to identifying your judgments, your criticisms of yourself (which are only the old stories that tell you your mind) to get away from this influence. Otherwise, you will react emotionally to thoughts that are harmful to you.

I hope this will help you begin to change your attitude and look towards your body. Of course, accepting your body and developing your self-awareness is not done overnight. There is no magic formula for that, a miracle solution. It is a question of daily renewing one's intention to take care of oneself and to treat oneself well. Wearing clothes of our size, going to this Zumba class, taking a bath, finding ourselves pretty today, resting when we are tired, sending our minds off when it tells us that we are not up to it, go to this date even if our body does not suit us.

Allow yourself to live well simply by appreciating yourself.

Trauma and your relationship with your body Possible causes of insecure attachment to negative emotions include poverty, domestic violence, lack of support (for example, if the family is incomplete, unlike a nuclear family (mother, father, and children), or a complex family that includes several generations of relatives - grandparents, aunts/uncles, and sometimes not relatives associated with this family, life in a foster family and conflict between parents. But one of the main factors of unreliable attachment to negative emotions is trauma. When it comes to attachment, trauma is very important; I'll tell you more about it.

A traumatic experience is one in which you feel threatened. Having been injured, you experienced a feeling of helplessness, extreme fear, or horror. Your body may have responded to the injury with a strong heartbeat, rapid breathing, trembling, dizziness, or other physical symptoms. Sometimes an injury involves some kind of event, such as a natural disaster or death in a family. Sometimes it can last for a period of time and include many events, for example, when you have been abused for weeks, months, or years. If you were constantly neglected when you grew up, if your basic needs were not met, this could also be an injury.

Injury has a number of consequences for the body. Experts believe that traumatic memories are "stored" in the body and can come up when you feel certain smells or tastes (including food), hear certain sounds, touch something vaguely familiar. Sometimes, on the contrary, some recall these memories by touching you in a certain way. You may not be aware of the connection between physical sensations and your trauma until these memories completely capture you in reality or in a dream. But when this happens, you may feel that the injury did not happen to you in the distant past, but is happening again right now.

If you have an old injury, you probably noticed that you are always in a state of "alert." Compared to others, during stress, you are easily overstrained and harder to calm down. Stress and your reaction to it can cause you to use food as a way to calm down or dull your senses.

How injury affects the brain

Insecure attachment and trauma have a significant effect on the brain. Experts are accustomed to believing that trauma mainly affects the mind, psyche, that is, the subjective experience of self-awareness, consciousness, and personality. Now it's clear that experiences like child abuse affects the brain itself. In fact, traumatic experiences affect the development of nerve connections in the brain and change them. Complete neglect or severe trauma can even affect brain size. Children's trauma occurs at a time when the brain develops very quickly, and life experience literally sculpts it. The development of the brain involves the formation of connections between nerve cells. And crucial to how exactly these connections are formed in the brain are relationships with the primary caregiver. Thus, happening again and again, positive experiences from communication with the teacher and the formation of a reliable attachment leave traces that help strengthen the sense of security and insecurity in the brain. If negative, stressful, or traumatic experiences are more common in your past, then traces remain in your brain that lead to feelings of self-doubt, shame, guilt, and insecurity.

Childhood trauma or the consequences of abuse can occur at any age and in a variety of ways: internally - like depression, anxiety, borderline personality disorder, suicidal thoughts, or post-traumatic stress. Outwardly - as aggressive behavior, impulsiveness, crime, dependence, or hyperactivity. Fortunately, the brain is able to change and heal over time. This ability is called ductility.

How trauma leads to food addiction
Trauma can lead not only to unreliable attachment but also ultimately to food dependence. If you survived an injury, your brain has evolved to help you survive, keeping you in a constant state of alertness, always awaiting the next kick or another mess. This may be one

of the reasons why you turn to food, alcohol, drugs, sex, or other means that help you calm down and relieve another feeling of tension. The brain has prepared you to quickly respond to the threat of stress, but for this, it has to release stress hormones (adrenaline and cortisol) from certain of its sites that do not allow other areas to develop, especially those that are responsible for common sense, control of impulses and others, higher function.

Perhaps you have already begun to understand that with the help of food you are trying to cope with anxiety or insecurity, the reason for which is the inability (in the absence of experience) to form reliable connections. Sometimes people become attached to food simply as their only friend. Or food becomes the only way for them to feel love or comfort. In the following exercise, check to see if your relationship with food matches the types of affection that you learned about in this chapter. For example, is your food attachment disorganized, rigid,or ambivalent?

Exercise 1

1.) Describe your relationship with food. Analyze whether it developed to fill the gap that has arisen as a result of unreliable attachment to a parent of another main caregiver (e.g., spouse, work). Ask yourself what is addictive in your relationship with the food process or with certain foods.

If in your childhood, you did not have a healthy relationship with the main caregiver, this may affect your relationship with food. However, these relationships can be changed. Sometimes a child without a healthy relationship with a primary caregiver may find a healthy relationship with a teacher, therapist, another family member, or close friend. And it happens that your first healthy attachment becomes a spouse or partner. This healthier relationship can be an example, a model of what a good relationship should be. Subsequently, this model can be used to change your relationship with food.

2.) Describe what three things you could transfer to your relationship with food that you modeled on any healthy relationships you have.

3.) Now name at least one action you can take to start changing your relationship with food.

An example: To bring more presence to my relationship with food, I turn off the TV while eating and listen to soothing music.

Hopefully, you will better understand how attachment problems can affect your relationship with food and lead to food addiction and food dependence. This understanding will only improve your relationship with food, which is not your enemy at all and is not the true cause of your problems with the food process. It is important that you understand what these reasons lie in because they also affect other areas of your life. If you have attachment problems, they also affect your intimate, friendly, and even working relationships. Do not let you feel intimacy with children, brothers/sisters, and reduce the overall quality of your life.

After solving problems with food addiction, you will notice after some time that the changes have spread to other areas of life, improving your relationship not only with food and the food process.

So far, you have analyzed your type of attachment and considered whether nutritional problems could be associated with it. In the exercise below, you combine all of these ideas to tell the story of your long-standing struggle with the food itself and its absorption process.

Exercise 2

Describe, starting with your earliest memories of food and gradually moving forward, to your current relationship with food, how you developed a food addiction.

An example: I have a photo where I'm probably three years old. I'm dressed in a pretty dress, on my feet - little white leather shoes with lacing, and in each hand - a big chocolate chip cookie. Realizing that I had a food addiction, I often thought about this photo and wondered: why are there two cookies? I couldn't take them myself. So, the mother gave it. Why didn't she limit me to one, but indulge my childhood greed?

I remember a lot of family holidays where I was given the opportunity to try something special. Preparing these dishes, my mother showed love for us, her family. Eating them, I showed her that I also love her. I remember, as soon as I began to get fat as a child, I was forbidden to eat certain foods. And they put me on my first diet when I was five.

Growing up, I always felt unprotected or unloved. But I continued to diet until fifty until I finally got tired of being always dissatisfied with my weight. And so, returning mentally to where my food addiction seems to have started, I recall those cookies (two! Too many!), and I understand that food can also serve as a way to convey love. But then, when I got fat, I was deprived of both the food that was taught to love and the love that was shown with food.

Whatever your own history of food addiction is, keep reminding yourself that, like the two-biscuit girly example, many factors have led to this problem. Entering the path of recovery, do not underestimate yourself. And remind yourself also that time and patience are required by any significant enterprise (and even more so). Your food addiction didn't develop in one night, and it won't leave you in one night. But witheach step, you will be closer and closer to the ultimate goal - getting rid of obsessive ideas about food and your body.

You are on the right track! Good luck!

Body appreciation scale

The most common method for estimating body mass is to calculate body mass index (BMI). However, you really need to say goodbye to the scales. Our weight fluctuates from day to day and from month to month according to our different biological rhythms. It actually gives very little information about our health, even though our society gives it a lot of importance. Besides, not weighing yourself, for many of us, leads to less judgment and guilt. To eat intuitively, one must relearn to listen to one's body, and by weighing oneself, one blurs intuition by judging us in front of what, socially, is "acceptable."

Notice and appreciate the bodily diversity that surrounds us. In the metro, in class or at work, pay attention to the diversity of appearances. I love to notice this diversity; I find it very beautiful. Many nutritionists use the analogy of dogs: there are all kinds of breeds, and we will never ask a German shepherd to look like a greyhound, so how do we justify this demand at the level of humans? By normalizing the diversity of bodies, we necessarily normalize ours. And it feels good!

Chapter 8:
Hyperphagia?

How is it going? Happiness, sadness, joy, melancholy, distress, suffering, anger, feelings of guilt, tension, doubt, vulnerability. Even though it is important to feel emotions, as noted, knowing how to manage them without using food as comfort is not always easy.

What is hyperphagia?

Hyperphagia, also known as binge eating, is the recurrent consumption of large amounts of food, accompanied by a feeling of loss of control. It is not followed by inappropriate compensatory behavior, such as induced vomiting or laxative abuse. The diagnosis is clinical.

More prevalent than anorexia and bulimia, hyperphagia, and especially binge eating disorder is now experiencing a meteoric rise and hits both men and women. Hyperphagia is characterized by uncontrolled rages of stuffing, orgies of food, without fasting, without vomiting. Shame is one of the symptoms of overeating;

the person usually eats in hiding.

Emotions: first causes of hyperphagia

We have all experienced negative emotions at home, in our environment, our self-esteem, at work, and outside. Learning to manage emotions is, therefore, very important for ourselves and our future.

Knowing what causes your negative emotions and what emotions you experience most often will allow you to immediately apply a strategy to interrupt them. So, what are these negative emotions that can quickly drag you into the spiral of hyperphagia?

Frustration when you feel trapped or stuck, unable to move forward.

The anxiety that can easily become uncontrollable and impact your mental health but also your productivity at work.

Anger, especially uncontrolled, is one of the most destructive emotions, and the most difficult to manage properly.

Discontent when an unpleasant situation is imposed on us daily. The disappointment/sadness that usually results in energy and morale at the lowest level with the fear of taking risks.

The hyperphagia, therefore, always begins with a feeling of malaise, which, by worsening it, can ruin a whole life. A situation often misunderstood both by the person concerned and those around him, until the famous crises followed by guilt.

One must know above all that a hyperphagic person is a person who does not see himself as she really is, with a false idea of herself. She usually feels: ugly, fat, incapable, useless, etc. Food becomes an outlet for "filling in the blanks." This is usually a top stage of emotional eating.

There are several different types of hyperphagia:

Overeating during the meal, which consists of eating very large quantities at the time of meals. Signals of satiety (sensation of gastric fullness and well-being, leading to the cessation of food intake) are delayed.

Then the second type of hyperphagia is characterized by repeated nibbling, without feeling hunger or appetite, and often related to boredom or anxiety.

There are also food compulsions that impulsively, brutally push to consume food or a category of foods.

Comes finally, binge eating, which is characterized by the instinctual absorption, in a very short time, of a great quantity of food.

The person in hyperphagia does not feel the need to induce vomiting to control his weight, which differentiates binge eating from true bulimia.

Emotional management and food compulsion: nervous hunger

Different from organic hunger - when your belly tells you that your body has a biological need for food - nervous or emotional hunger is the signal of your "ghost" belly.

To be clearer, we have 2 bellies: a real and a fake. It is this last one that sends a signal of "hunger" when disturbing emotions come to cross the threshold of your conscience.

With bad management of his emotions, when the nervous hunger is felt, one feels then obliged to fill to stifle the expression of his emotions. A hunger is so powerful that you lose control until you steal and hide food even in the middle of the night! The need to open the fridge several times, to take a look in his cupboards, without being really hungry. Does this context speak to you?

Factors triggering nervous hunger
Nervous hunger is a hunger that accompanies inner malaise. We often talk about compulsive overeating. It is triggered in different ways: situations - places - triggering events.

How stress affects your body and leads to disordered eating
Stressful work meeting, boring family meeting, a doctor's appointment, a sporting event, an invitation to the restaurant, an uninteresting workday. The trigger varies depending on the person.

Your boss, your spouse, who often returns late at night, a parent, your children can trigger in you a nervous hunger by a simple look, a word, or a heavy silence.

What you need to know is that emotional hunger is quite normal, and this translates to birth. A crying baby immediately stops crying when his mother feeds him. The food soothes it. From childhood, therefore, we associate food with survival, love, and peace of mind.

If the need for food and well-being has been properly met since childhood, there will be a tendency to associate comfort with food. On the other hand, if they have not been satisfied, food and love will be linked. It is often for this reason that most people are experiencing a disappointment in love rush over food to make up for the lack. The food then became an object of love.

Remember: By constantly pressing the food button to stifle your discomfort or "ignite" a feeling of instant but short-term well-being, it is that you have not finished living the nostalgia of your childhood.

No wonder then that you are tenaciously clinging to your emotional cravings! Stopping these food compulsions has gradually become for you a too scary prospect ... that will have to change if you finally want to "grow up."

Freeing yourself from your emotional hunger: why are diets not effective?

Diets generally recommend reducing dietary intakes and following certain well-defined rules. The goal of diets is to control their eating habits.

For people who are dependent on food, this is impossible. Why? Because their need to eat is too strong, uncontrollable. Food is a quick and easy way for them to "defuse" too intense or anxiety-provoking emotions. A policy of the ostrich face life.

An infernal circle where recognizing one's existence is not enough, nor is the will. So what to do?

How to learn the joy of eating well

It's not like changing drinks or clothes. Changing a behavioral eating disorder requires a real introspection: analyze what is happening in your life, confront you with what you want to avoid at all costs while eating. This is the only and only way to get you out of this infernal circle!

Regaining control over food by surpassing feelings of helplessness

It is normal to feel helpless in the face of events that have been out of control for a long time. But for the "emotional eaters," as they are called, this feeling of helplessness can be overcome by identifying exactly the causes. This can be:

- impotence to manage your doubts about yourself;
- helplessness to be satisfied with your life;
- an inability to ensure your own safety;
- helplessness to assume your independence;
- impotence to fill the void that you feel internally.
- feelings of helplessness that translate into an uncontrollable desire for food.

The hole - Brain and emotions: a primitive story

It must also be known that the part of the brain that processes emotions is the limbic system. Many studies suggest that this part of the brain has evolved fairly early in the history of mankind, making it very primitive.

The reason why an emotional response is often very simple, but very intense, often based on the need to survive. Strongly related to memory and experience, the emotional response to the same stimulus is, therefore, often the same.

For example, if a movie made you very scared, seeing it again will awaken your feeling of fear unless you have worked this emotion to not have to relive that. What you need to remember is that no matter how hard you try to change your eating habits, no matter how sincere your promise to take control of yourself, without real introspection, you will not be able to control your emotional hunger for long.

And if you cannot change despite your several trials, it's because food has become an automatic appeasement response to the difficulties you've encountered in your life. Because it is the emotional hunger that makes intuitive diets fail as well as denial.

Solving your inner conflicts will allow you to lose weight and permanently silence your emotional hunger!

Chapter 9:
Food Confusion Leads to
Disordered Eating

Sometimes people are surprised that their digestive system reacts strangely to the consumption of certain foods. Moreover, there is no doubt about their quality and natural origin. Most often, in such cases, the body reacts to an unsuccessful combination of foods included in the diet. Already in the distant past, people understood the importance of separate nutrition, and this principle underlies many diets and has a large number of adherents.

History reference

The incompatibility of some products with others has been known for a long time, as evidenced by the works of the ancient Roman physician Celsus. Even Avicenna warned that certain food combinations are harmful to the human body. Studies of the famous academician Pavlov in the field of the enzymatic function of the stomach showed a change in its composition during the assimilation of various food products. Modern nutritionists recommend a separate diet to reduce excess weight and just to maintain the health of the body.

Factors that influence fullness - Process of digestion

The digestion rate of each product is different. If it takes about 20 minutes to assimilate the apple, the meat will be digested much longer. If you finish a hearty dinner with some fruit, then its assimilation will be inhibited, since the food eaten before that will be digested first. Thus, instead of fruits benefiting the human body, they will rot in the intestines.

The digestion process is not limited to the active participation of gastric juice. The assimilation of food occurs under the influence of saliva, gall bladder, pancreas, as well as bacteria present in the body. If any of these links fail, the process changes.

Product incompatibility reason

For the absorption of certain foods, certain enzymes are used. For example, protein food is digested in an acidic environment, carbohydrate - in an alkaline one. During the chemical interaction of these media, a neutralization reaction occurs, which increases the duration of the digestive process, and leads to an increase in energy expenditure for its implementation. As a result of taking products incompatible with each other, a person feels heaviness in the stomach, and his performance decreases for a long time.

Many problems of the gastrointestinal tract arise due to a violation of the basics of proper nutrition. This is due to the fact that the use of incompatible products increases the load on the digestive system and reduces its efficiency.

Foods that increase fullness - The value of the right combination of products

The main function of the gastrointestinal tract is the digestion of food of any origin, both plant and animal. In this process, its microflora is involved, which ultimately determines its quality and the final result. This can be a quick and effective assimilation of food or a slow process in which rotting products occur.

The qualitative and quantitative composition of microflora is diverse and numerous. At the same time, some types of microorganisms prevail, while others are in a depressed state. Depending on the nature of food and the rate of metabolic processes, their species composition is determined. Stabilization of microflora occurs if the diet includes natural products in the right combination.

Irregular eating or overeating leads to disruption of the gastrointestinal tract. Food that stays in the intestines for a long time becomes the food of putrefactive bacteria, which produce poisons and toxins in the course of their life. These compounds penetrate the liver and kidneys, after which the whole organism is poisoned by them, which leads to the development of many diseases. These lead to depression and anxiety, and guess? Emotional eating. It becomes a cycle.

The Shelton principle

Herbert Shelton made a significant contribution to the creation of the fundamentals of separate nutrition, on which many diets are based, and proposed the principles of simple nutrition. His idea is that you should observe the uniformity of food in one meal.

According to Shelton, an additional effect can be obtained by using fasting, which caused a storm of indignation from colleagues. Despite the fact that when using his methods, there were cases of cure from various ailments, the doctor went to jail.

To simplify the perception of information, the scientist brought information about food compatibility into a table, which is currently widely used. Shelton also recommends consuming no more than three different products, and ideally one.

The Hay theory

Howard Hay's research was based on the principles that Shelton formulated. Subsequently, the scientist developed his own theory, according to which all food products are divided into three classes: protein, carbohydrate, and neutral. In addition, Hay is a supporter of the rejection of certain categories of food and called for the elimination of refined foods from the diet.

According to the nutritionist, people eat a lot of foods that lead to the predominance of an acidic environment, which causes many different diseases. From here, according to Hay, the conclusion follows that you need to eat food, which leads to the appearance of an alkaline reaction - vegetables, fruits, and sour-milk products.

Moreover, the amount of "alkaline" food should exceed four times the proportion of "acidic."

A modern view of the problem

At present, nutritionists conditionally subdivide all products into ten types. The main difference from the classical version of the classification is the separation of products into moderately compatible and incompatible ones. This is due to the fact that the starch content in some products is high, while in others, it is insignificant.

1.) Fruit

Fruits are absorbed in a relatively short time. At the same time, the digestion of acidic fruit in the stomach is faster and sweeter - slower. According to nutritionists, it is better to use them as a separate dish 1-1.5 hours before a meal, and at least 3 hours should pass after the previous meal. In addition, they should not be a component of dessert. The same rule applies to fruit juices.

Other types of fruits, cereals, and sour-milk products are combined with sweet fruits.

2.) Semisweet or semi-sweet foods

Greens and sour-milk are suitable for this category of food. Due to the different rates of assimilation, semisweet, or semi-sour foods do not combine wellwith meat, fish, cereals and legumes, and foods containing large amounts of starch.

These are not combined with any other types of products, as the assimilation of the latter is inhibited. The food in the stomach begins to rot, and as a result, bloating occurs.

3.) Sour foods

They can be combined in the fruits of their group and other types of sour foods. In addition, they can be used along with dairy products and various derivatives of milk. High-protein and starch-rich foods, cereals, and legumes, vegetables do not combine with sour foods.

4.) Vegetables

Some vegetable crops combine well with other foods and with representatives of their group. This is due to the fact that they promote digestion and contribute to the acceleration of the assimilation of a variety of foods. Vegetables and fruits are an undesirable tandem, but there are exceptions to this rule. Milk and vegetables are an unacceptable food combination.

There are a number of vegetables that are worse combined with other foods, but starchy foods, other representatives of vegetable crops, fats, and greens are great for them. Cheese also goes well with such vegetables, but you should refuse to use milk and fruit with them.

5.) Starchy foods

This category includes most crops and products made from them, as well as corn and potatoes. They go well with greens, fats, and vegetables. If fats are present, then it is desirable that greens go along with them.

6.) Proteins

The assimilation of protein products is better if you eat greens and vegetables with them, which, in addition, remove the toxins present in them. With such food, it is best to combine fats and greens to enhance their absorption. Protein foods cannot be combined with starchy foods, fruits, and sugars. An exception is the food composition, which includes derivatives of milk, nuts, and fruits.

7.) Food incompatible with milk

It should be understood that milk is food, so before it enters the intestines, it needs to curl up in the stomach under the influence of enzymes. When the milk enters at the same time as another meal, the mucous membrane of the stomach is enveloped, which violates its normal activity. Milk is incompatible with almost all products. The exception is fruits, but this combination may not be suitable for everyone.

8.) Greens

All green plants that are suitable for consumption are ideally combined with any other products except milk. Greens, according to nutritionists, should be present on the table every day. Most of all, it is beneficial in the use of starchy and protein foods. In this case, greens help to digest such products and neutralize toxins. In addition, it is rich in vitamins and has beneficial effects on the muscles of the intestines.

9.) Fats

The products of this group are distinguished by the fact that they inhibit the production of gastric juice, and soften the effects of products that are poorly combined with each other. Fats with herbs, vegetables, and starchy foods are combined in the best way. They are fully compatible with various fruits.

Sugar and fats are an unsuccessful combination, which should be discarded since the effects of inhibition of digestion are manifested to the maximum. It is advisable not to use a mixture of vegetable and animal fats.

10.) Sugar

Protein and starchy foods, combined with sugar, leads to the development of the fermentation process, which makes the products less useful. Sugar should be consumed separately from other foods or completely excluded from the diet.

Among all types of sugars, honey is the only exception. In a small amount, it can be used with any products, since it inhibits the processes of fermentation and decay.

A wrong combination affects your system and leads to disordered eating. This is because your body will ask for more foods to counter the effects of your error. Simple, just avoid any such errors!

Chapter 10:
Addressing
Cravings

Everyone who enters the battle with food addiction knows that defeating it is not easy. Understanding the mechanisms of work of food addiction will bring you closer to getting rid of it, healing and losing weight.

If you tried to refuse junk food, then you know that it is very difficult to do this. To understand how to get rid of food dependence, you need to understand the mechanism of its work. As a rule, dependence is directed to certain products, you know that this product is harmful to your health and figure, but you cannot refuse it.

The issue of treating food addiction is not only willpower. The brain can perceive unhealthy food as a reward, while food begins to work as a drug - to bring pleasure from eating and "joy" in case of failure in other areas of life. When using a product that gives the brain the properties of a reward, neurotransmitters are produced, one of the most powerful is dopamine. Over time, less dopamine is produced per serving of the product, with dopamine tolerance, people begin to eat more junk food. No wonder food addiction is equated with the strongest physical addictions.

It is important to learn to distinguish hunger for food cravings. Craving for food comes suddenly, regardless of whether you are hungry or just ate. It can also wake up under the influence of a trigger; for example, you smell baking and want to eat it immediately. An emotional state can also become a trigger, with stress, depression, people feel an increased need for dopamine and try to get it with food stimulation. It is impossible to understand how to overcome food dependence, knowing your triggers; they need to be studied and eliminated.

If you realize that you are using food as a reward or comfort, then look for alternative ways to please yourself. At the very beginning, not a single stimulation will bring such an effect as a portion of ice cream or a donut, but over time the brain will reconsider its attitude.

The danger of food dependence in the absence of self- control, it is impossible to satisfy food cravings, while remaining moderate. Overeating leads to obesity, circulatory disorders, and other internal problems. Succumbing to cravings, a person who is addicted to food feels that he is better, but in fact, he is much worse.

Many experts recommend completely abandoning drug products or alcohol as a cure, as this will only create another branch of dependence.

Overcoming food addiction, it will not be possible to limit the use of unhealthy food; this is the same as offering a smoker to smoke, not a whole cigarette, but a third.
This will not work, but only exacerbate addiction, cause more serious physical and psychological problems.

When choosing a tactic of restriction, dependent people usually adhere to it only for those around them; that is, they eat a few tablespoons of ice cream in public, and when left alone, they eat up the entire tray. This behavior leads to a decrease in self-esteem, protracted deep depression, and increased dependence.

To get rid of food dependence, there are no miracle cures and universal methods. It is important to understand yourself, to analyze the causes of development, to identify triggers. When food addiction is overgrown with eating disorders, the ailment becomes a mental disorder. If working on yourself does not bring results, you should seek the professional help of a psychologist or psychiatrist; a specialist will choose a way to get rid of food dependence for you personally.

Meditation to overcome an obsessive craving for food

Noticed that we often eat, not to satisfy hunger by nourishing our body with the elements he needs, but to relieve stress, enjoy, drown out the pain, or longing? Does no solution seem to work for you?

In Kundalini Yoga, there is a meditation that allows a person to learn to control their appetite.

Pose: simple, straight spine, stretched up. Mudra:

Right thumb closes the right nostril.

Respiration: Inhalation through the left nostril, delay in inhalation for a maximum time. Exhale through the left nostril and hold on the exhale for the same time as on the inspiration. Keep breathing this way for 31 minutes.

"If you practice this breathing technique for 31 minutes every day for 90 days, you can cure the most advanced cases. Just don't overdo it. Breathing through the left nostril should be deep and slow, without pressure on the diaphragm. This will force the left half of the primitive brain to take control and counteract the impulse that says, "I have to eat."

This means that if you activate the one channel that controls the satisfaction of your survival needs to make a decision about the choice and quantity of food, then you will eat, so much, and exactly what is needed for the effective functioning of the body.

This is an incredibly significant achievement, because, ultimately, it will save you from a huge number of problems with physical and mental health.

Distracted eating
To lose weight and feel full, doctors and nutritionists say that you need to focus on it (your food) with every meal.

It doesn't matter if you cycle during lunch, carry out errands, inhale breakfast on the road or relax in front of the TV for lunch; multitasking while eating can be effective and even enjoyable. But you also may have noticed how easy it is to overeat when you are not fully focused on food and hunger levels. And when it comes to weight gain, this extra, distracting method of eating food can pile up quickly.

The solution is simple but effective: sit back, focus on your food and enjoy it to the fullest, says the director of bariatric surgery at Stanford University. The doctor recommends evaluating every aspect of your meal: looking at food in different ways, enjoying "its beauty - its color, its smell, its cooking." According to him, the assessment of your food can really change your feelings during meals and after it. In addition to giving you more time to tune in to hunger signals, you will also feel more contented and less likely to reach your next snack.

Paying close attention to your food will help you eat more slowly, which is associated with smaller waist sizes, as well as lower BMI and obesity. You will also feel less bloated. And it makes sense: if you slow down to enjoy every bite, the food will take you more time, and you will definitely understand when it is time to stop.

So eat more carefully - easier said than done, right? Well, I think that the food is so delicious that it makes sense to enjoy it as much as possible. Close your eyes and allow yourself to truly appreciate all the delicacies in each fork, even if it is "just" a salad or chicken cooked with food. You will avoid overeating, and you can see some benefits in weight loss, but, even better, you will feel completely satisfied and really full after each meal.

Chapter 11:

Natural Detox: What It Is and How to Speed Up the Process

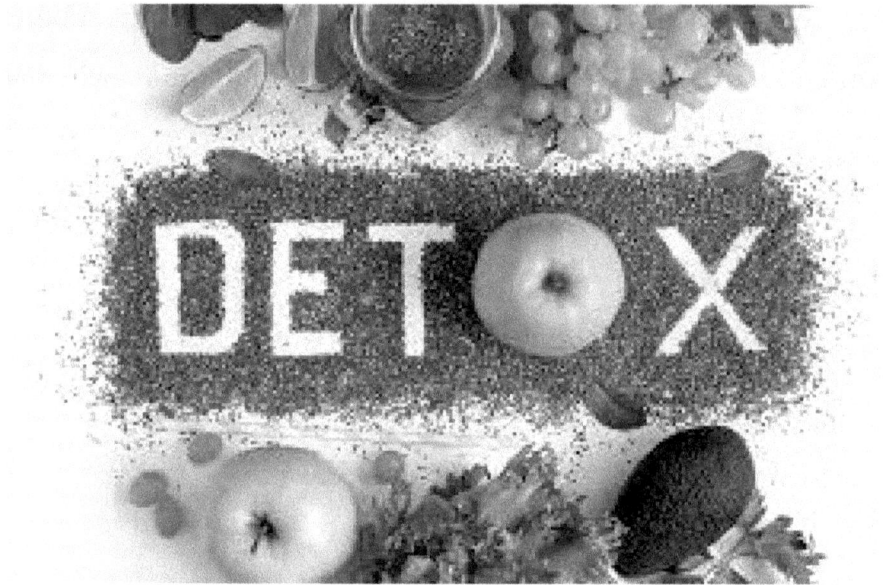

All kinds of detox programs conquer the world. Starvation, living on water, juice detox, unloading diets, etc. How not to get lost in a sea of information and not harm yourself with promising programs to cleanse the body, which often costs a lot of money? I offer information about who needs it, why, and how to conduct a detox program at home yourself. In this chapter, you will get a guide to detox programs that you can try at home without negative health consequences.

Detox program

We are able to get rid of toxins that constantly get into our body with food or from the environment by nature; however, helping our body with simple methods can speed up and improve this process.

Residents of large cities are the main objects of influence of many toxic factors that abound in the urban environment. The idea of controlling their volume in 80 cases out of a hundred is doomed to failure. But the idea of helping the body protect itself from them by all available means can lead to positive (and most pleasant: physically tangible) results.

If the detoxification function of the body is not in order, both appearance and health may suffer. Our body independently and continuously filters everything that it receives from us, displacing waste and toxins. Each cell can carry out its own detoxification and get rid of environmental and metabolic debris. This is the so-called natural detoxification. You can only trust this complex and natural system. And knowing how it works, you can help her and speed up the process of updating the body.

Detox through the lymphatic system

The human lymphatic system resembles the secondary circulatory system, which forms an extensive network of organs and tissues throughout the body. Itssignificance is enormous: it is she who is responsible for the circulation of all fluids in the body and ridding the body of the burden of unnecessary or harmful elements (such as white blood cells, bacteria, viruses, and toxins). Failure of this miraculous system can lead to a chronic feeling of fatigue, decreased immunity, and increased slowness. Preventing it with simple methods is pretty simple:

1.) Add activity: physical activity creates pressure that increases the intensity of fluid circulation in the body. Walking, cycling, yoga - there are enough options for sports activities for every taste. The main thing is to maintain the dynamics of the body.

2.) Meditation plus deep breathing: stress negatively affects the health of the lymphatic system. A conscious fifteen-minute meditation for every day will maintain the balance of the nervous system, and the contraction of the muscles, which is activated by deep breathing, will create additional pressure and normalize the circulation of fluid in the body.

3.) Use a brush and a comb: they will help to arrange an effective drainage session for your skin. For this, both ordinary bristles and loofah are suitable. We try in the morning before an invigorating shower.

4: For sleep, choose spacious clothing: at night, the detox of the body is intense and reaches its maximum between 10 o'clock in the evening and 2 o'clock in the morning. Tight underwear, compressing areas of the lymph nodes, can negatively affect the effectiveness of night detox. So the freer your robe during the hours of sleep, the healthier the awakening of the body the next day.

Detox through sweating

Your skin is the largest organ to remove toxins. If you do physical exercises about three times a week for at least 20 minutes, then you will optimize the detox potential of your pores. Sweating helps to remove metals such as lead, mercury, cadmium from the body, so it's good to take a steam bath after playing sports. Studies have also shown that with sweat, the body gets rid of numerous endocrine disruptors that interfere with the normal functioning of hormones.

Removing harmful decomposition products and excess chemical elements from the body is not the only useful function of perspiration. The usual sweat contains antibiotics (in special proteins), stem cells, as well as prebiotics, which helps to heal the skin, increase the efficiency of cell metabolism, as well as the removal of pathogenic bacteria, often leading to acne. In the course of evolution, the human body has become a real guru in the field of detox.

Detox through urination and stool

The kidneys are a unique pair of filtering organs that are responsible for the most important channel for flushing out toxins and impurities from the blood. Healthy kidneys do everything to ensure a balance of salts and fluids in the body, maintain normal blood pressure and acid-base balance. This system of organs faithfully and faithfully serves the detox of the body throughout a person's life. Here are the treasured ways in which you will do them a great service in this difficult matter:

1.) Drink plenty of water: the kidneys need water to secrete urine, and it is the main "excreting" substance of our body. A low level of its generation can lead to the formation of "stones" in the kidneys. To prevent all unpleasant malfunctions in their work, just do not forget to drink 3.7 (for women) and 4.0 (for men) liters of clean liquid per day.

2. Recommended foods: foods high in calcium, seaweed, freshly squeezed juices, cranberries, and grapes will be ideal items in your diet, especially if you are serious about cleaning your kidneys.

3.) Use herbal supplements: omega-3, vitamin B-6, and potassium citrate — the list can be expanded after consulting a doctor.

4.) Formed stools once or twice a day: one of the best ways to rid the body of toxins. You can help the body in this process by increasing the intake of fiber - fresh vegetables, fruits, healthy cereals, legumes, whole grains.

Detox through the liver
This body is one of the leaders in multitasking. It has a sensitive waste filtration and disposal system. In the liver, the most important process of the neutralization of

substances brought by lymph occurs. The liver cleanses our blood, and in order to help it, you can take the following simple measures (however, this statement is purely individual):

1.) Control your body mass index: Refrain from regular overeating, frequent drinking of alcohol, and strive for regular physical training.

2.) Avoid actions with a high risk of negative consequences: unprotected sex with different sexual partners, drugs - a classic list for this item, which any doctor will not fail to mention.

3.) Know your risk factors: heredity or excessive alcohol consumption can cause liver problems or simply activate them. Some diseases may not be felt for many years and may not come up at the right time in your life. Diagnosis and diagnosis again: do not be too lazy to undergo an examination if you feel something is amiss.

Build good gut function

To conclude this chapter, I will share with you five express tips to improve your gut function for the ultimate detox. I am sharing with you proven methods that will help improve the work of the digestive tract.

Nourishment as self-care

To get started, adjust your diet. Try to eat at the same time, 5-6 times a day in small portions. In this case, do not take long breaks between meals, a maximum of 3-4 hours. Chew each piece of food thoroughly and do not drink food with water or other drinks. For better assimilation of food, it is worth drinking half an hour before and half an hour after eating.

The same rule applies to fresh fruits: do not eat them for dessert after the main meal. They can cause digestive disorders, lead to stagnation and fermentation of the eaten.

Self-care nourishment plan

In the morning on an empty stomach, drink a glass of warm, clean water, preferably with lemon juice, to easily and naturally awaken your digestive system. Warm water on an empty stomach perfectly rinses the stomach and improves the functioning of the pancreas, and lemon juice will relieve the unpleasant sensations of bloating, belching, and heartburn. If you suffer from gastritis, add 1 tsp to morning water instead of lemon juice. You can also add honey.

Such "honey vodka" improves the production of gastric juice and also promotes the regeneration of tissues of the mucous membrane, which is damaged in gastritis.

Enrich your daily diet with fiber-rich foods. It is like a brush that cleanses the gastrointestinal tract, absorbing harmful substances and sweeping undigested food debris. The use of fiber can prevent constipation, dysbiosis, and obesity, as well as normalize the function of beneficial bacteria, improve the absorption of the necessary trace elements and create optimal conditions for the movement of food through the digestive tract. For this purpose, it is worth at least 60% to enrich your diet with fresh fruits, vegetables, and herbs.

Do not forget about the general cleaning of the intestines. After all, daily accumulate of harmful substances in it, undigested food debris, pathogenic microflora must be regularly disposed of. It is the clutter of the intestine that gives rise to many diseases.

For bowel cleansing, hydrotherapy can be carried out in the clinic 1-2 times a year. And you can clean up wellat home, using an enema, Epsom salt or castor oil for this. It is also recommended to arrange weekly fasting days when you will only drink juices, water, or herbal teas.

Well, of course, for the gastrointestinal tract to work perfectly, you need to move a lot. Movement is life! Any physical activity, whether it is simply walking, jogging on the street or weight training, and cardio training in the gym, improves intestinal motility. Apply these simple ways to improve the digestive tract, and you will almost immediately feel a surge of strength, energy, and health, and diseases will bypass you.

What about allergies and medical conditions?
In this case, it is safe to exempt any foods that cause you discomfort or are proven to have a negative impact on your health.

Chapter 12:
The Ultimate Path Toward Healing From Eating Disorders - Knock-Out Tips

What do when you lose passion and purpose Without a goal and passion, people often succumb to anger and frustration; they feel miserable and worthless. Everything becomes inharmonious: words diverge from deeds, thoughts - with words, the body feels uncomfortable, and the psyche surrenders.

You cannot find passion and purpose sitting on the couch. This is a huge job to do. It is necessary to immerse yourself in the depths of self-reflection, forget yourself for a while and study yourself. But for this, we need tools that will help and direct in the right direction. This chapter will talk about the best of them.

You need to start by knowing yourself. Below you will find a series of questions that will help you better know yourself. Allow enough time and dig as deep as possible:

- What am I good at by nature?
- How can I apply my talents?

- What makes me feel good?

- What fears make me pleasantly excited?

- In what types of activities do I most often show my creative thinking?

- What tasks interest me the most?

- What do I like to read about?

- What do I like to talk about?

- What would I regret if I hadn't tried?

- What would I like to teach others?

- What help and advice do people usually ask me?

- What am I most grateful for?

- What would I do for free all my life?

- What kind of life do I want to live?

- What will they remember me for?

- How do I measure success?

- What is the purpose of my life? What is my passion?

How to find purpose and passion in your life

If, after answering these questions, there is still a lot of doubt about the purpose and passion of your life, you need to broaden your horizons a bit. It is possible that up to this point you lived in your comfort zone, took a little risk and had a narrow range of positive emotions: all this in total could not give the inner spark that every person needs so much to catch on with a strong desire to change his life and achieve great successes.

Therefore, I advise you to devote the next week of your life to find yourself. This means exploring the world, looking for a wide variety of hobbies, reading unusual books, and meeting unique people.

You need to get out of the notorious comfort zone. This means not only traveling and testing oneself in the outside world, but also in the inside. For example, start a diary, read affirmations, work with your thoughts.

Getting to know your biological hunger

Among the issues addressed, that of the difference between biological hunger and emotional hunger. In preview, check out the below information to learn to dissociate them.

Distinguishing between thoughts and hunger cues

Your hunger is biological if...

- it develops little by little;
- you can wait to eat to be soothed;
- you pay attention to the quality and quantity of what you are tasting, and you stop to satiety;
- you savor what you taste;

- you enjoy a carrot, a salad or a tomato;
- after eating, you feel good.

Your hunger is emotional if...
- it arises in an intense and sudden way;
- you must eat immediately to be satisfied;
- you engulf more than you eat, and continue even if you are no longer hungry;
- you stumble on fatty and sweet foods rather than on a stream of steamed fish, for example.

If at birth, the hunger is emotional, you learn, normally, growing up to manage your emotions to regulate your internal mood. When this regulation is not made, food becomes the norm to extinguish its discomfort, but comfort is short-lived, resulting in a repetition of food intake. To get out of this vicious circle, it is importantto rehabilitate food education.

How? By explaining that eating is a pleasure, a conviviality, a sharing, and not only the intake of food substances. Any prolonged increase in food will resultin weight gain, hence the need to learn to manage emotions and to reclaim signs of hunger and satiation through long internal work.

Learning to say no

In our age of the Internet, technology, and a glut of information and goods, we are endlessly offered something. And if we don't want to become gluttons in the broadest sense of the word, it's important to be able to answer some sentences, "thank you, no." Let's start learning this with mindfulness and selectivity in food. I want to talk about how to politely refuse if you are offered food, but you do not want or cannot eat it.

I am a plus-size person, I often attend events, and the hospitable organizing hosts almost always want to feed me. Because of my high growth and strong physique, it always seems to people around that I eat a lot, but it's not. I don't go on diets for the sake of thinness, but I follow the intuitive diet to preserve the beauty of the skin, it is my work tool. Therefore, I often have to say the phrase "thank you, no" for food, and I can do it so that no one is offended.

The rules of etiquette come to the rescue. Everything in the world is changing, but cheers! - these rules remain the same island of stability, although - what a pity! - they are not taught at school. What to do if you were invited to a social event or a dinner party, and you should be selective in food?

- Let me offer you a sturgeon?

- No! I can't eat fish! I'm allergic to it ... Yes ... Cramps begin.

This, of course, cannot be said. Do not talk about your diseases, allergies, diets, and what kind of storm will happen in your stomach if you eat this pizza and drink it with this juice.

What should you do, especially if you are full?
To begin with, think about whether you can completely give up going to an event - may be not going to be easier than worrying about food all evening. Can you? Do this in advance, no later than two days before the designated date. If refusal for some reason is not possible, go to dinner, but follow a few rules there.

1. Flatly refuse to eat. It's better to have something on the plate and from time to time to twist the plug in your hands than to say loudly that today you are a no-no.

2. During the buffet, hold a full glass of water in your hand. So you are not bored, and others see that you have something at hand.

3. Avoid other overeaters - they will definitely advise you to eat something. In extreme cases, if the adviser still catches up with you, crossing your fingers behind your back, lie that you have already tried it.

4. Refuse shortly and benevolently. You can politely and quietly say so. In this case, it's more correct, tactful, and safer to say a short "thank you, no" with a smile, instead of the aggressive "I don't want!"

5. Give the right signals. Put a few appetizers on the plate for the look. It is unlikely that someone will closely monitor how the food goes to your mouth and how much you ate. At the same time, when there is food left on the plate, they don't add it to you yet. Is the waiter serving the table? Great, it's quite acceptable to give him a sign: put the cutlery in a corner - this means a break in food, horizontally - the food was excellent, vertically - you finished eating.

What distinct aromas are appealing?

After extensive research in the 1990s, biologists began to understand better how the sensors and chemicals in the body respond to the effects of smell. This research has opened many minds to a concept that ancient civilizations discovered long ago: smell can have a remarkable effect on human emotion and mood.

Based on the unique chemical profile of each food smell, we know that each will stimulate a specific emotional response. However, as two people are not the same, each individual can receive distinct benefits for their own well-being. Our reactions to flavors and food smells are based on environmental indicators, past experiences, personal preferences, and even our unique genetic makeup. Because of these individual factors, not all users will have the same psychological reaction to the same smells.

Identify the emotion you may be feeling on the basis of particular food smell. Give in to the concept of intuitive eating and indulge yourself freely. Also, eliminate all guilt while you eat the "forbidden" foods. Over time, your body will get less and less interested in such foods.

Chapter 13:

Eating as Sacred Time: Create the Optimal Eating Environment

Eating is an automatism for all; however, it is a much more complex act. In fact, eating not only serves to nourish one's body, but also to indulge oneself, to share with others and to feel integrated into a community (through the food culture), or even to feel good when one is under "tension" (psychological pressure).

The way we eat (rhythm, quantities, choices) is influenced by our education, our financial resources, beliefs. The quantities needed by our body are normally regulated by our unconscious brain, the hypothalamus, which also manages respiration. The elements that allow this regulation are hunger and satiation are signals emitted by the body (internal food signals). Hearing them and respecting them is the best guarantee of a stable weight (or a slimming aid in case of excess weight). Eating in a comfortable environment is a failsafe way of being able to feel your internal signals better. This must be sought at all costs.

Hunger and or satiety can be difficult to recognize, especially when you are under a lot of stress, when you are overwhelmed by emotions, or when you reject the comfort of an optimal eating environment.

Why satisfaction and pleasure are important Having fun while eating is not a source of weight gain; on the contrary, because this pleasure based on the sensations, food allows to better perceive the internal food signals. It is, therefore, advisable not to censor this pleasure and to let its food feelings fully express itself when food is in the mouth.

The more we are attentive to the pleasure brought by this moment of tasting, the more the quantity to be satisfied will be less.

The more we forbid this pleasure, the more we enter a tense relationship with the diet that promotes the irresistible urges to eat (food urges) and the risk of weight gain. This censorship favored by diets is known as "cognitive restriction."

Have fun while eating:

- by varying the flavors, the food, the methods of preparation, the presentations, making the meal a moment of conviviality;

- keeping fat and / or sweet foods, but keep in mind that it takes little to be full;

- be aware that you can use food to manage stress and personal difficulties (which can lead to eating beyond the needs of the body).

The importance of eating slowly and mindfully What you put on your plate is important. However, the way one takes one's meals is also important. However, socialization and the environment in which we find ourselves lead us to behave less and less spontaneously. In other words, we use less the physiological signals of hunger and satiety to conform to the customs of life in society (completely emptying one's plate, eating at fixed times).

Eat in peace, take the time to chew, to pay attention to your feelings, and eat with your 5 senses. Eat with pleasure: vary the flavors, the food, the modes of preparation, the presentation of food - make the meal a moment of conviviality. This slow and mindful eating pattern helps you to feel full satiety (when hunger is gone before the stomach is "tense").

What works with kids and teens?

You have probably noticed that some children eat little and others a lot. This is normal behavior. Indeed, babies and young children are specialists in listening to their signals of hunger and satiety! They can, among other things, choose not to eat because they are simply no longer hungry; a habit that often tends not to be respected in adults. For this reason, you are in some way conditioned to force them to finish their plate.

Your role as a parent is to choose the foods that will make up the meal, decide on the mealtime, and finally help your children identify their hunger and satiety signals. This is the best way to get them to consume the amount of food they need for growth.

What does true hunger, false hunger, satiety mean in a child?
In a natural way, the child eats the amount of food he needs. Children have different needs, and those of only one child vary from day to day. So you cannot guess for him the amount of food he needs. He is the intuitive eater! He eats at mealtimes when he is hungry and stops eating when he is no longer hungry. This is because he listens to his body, which gives him signals of hunger and satiety.

Hunger indicates that the body needs food to function well. The real hunger occurs gradually by gurgling, a hollow feeling in the stomach, decreased energy and concentration, irritability, and impatience. These signals do not deceive! On the other hand, a false hunger is manifested by a desire to eat, caused essentially by sensory stimulation (sight, smell, the evocation of appetizing food, emotions) or the fact of wanting to be rewarded (gluttony!).

In contrast, satiety is the disappearance of hunger. The child feels satiety when he regains his energy and has a full stomach after eating. For your part, you will notice that the child is less hungry when he begins to play with his food, slows down the rate at which he eats or when he wants to get up from the table.

How to recognize the signs of hunger and satiety at for toddlers who do not speak yet
Pay attention to behaviors. If he is hungry, he nibbles his hands; he becomes irritable, his belly gurgles. If he has eaten enough, he turns his head to protest, throws his spoon on the ground, and drops food on the floor.

How to recognize the signs of hunger and satiety in older children
You can help a child listen to his hunger and satiety signals by asking him what he feels before a meal. After eating, repeat the exercise and compare the answers so that the child understands how he feels when he is hungry and when he is no longer hungry.

Here are some sample questions to help the child eat intuitively:

- How do you know you're hungry?
- Do you have a small, medium, or big hunger?
- Are you still hungry?
- How do you know you have eaten enough?

Repeat for him to eat slowly and chew well, and show him the example. Thus, the child will realize that he is a master of the amount of food he eats. In addition, he will guide you on the size of the portions to put on his plate at the time of serving. Give him also the opportunity to serve again if he is hungry.

The behaviors to avoid with children during the meal
Adults can sometimes encourage children to finish eating even when they are no longer hungry. We must, therefore, avoid the following behaviors:

- Use food to comfort, calm, or distract a child.
- Ban food on the menu.
- Insist that he eat or finish his plate.
- Be proud of him if he is eating such a quantity of food.

The ability to recognize the hunger or satiety can be lost if you force the child to eat or when used to eat surrounded by several distractions (television, tablet, toy, etc.). Other factors may come into play, such as the availability of a favorite food, fear of lack of food, desire to please, boredom, or different emotions.

The child is then more likely to consume too much or not enough food in relation to his real needs. Make him eat at the table, without distraction. Meals and snacks are great opportunities for family fun. You can make the dining atmosphere pleasant (an optimal environment), all without forcing to eat.

In short, sharing responsibilities between your child and you allows him to listen to his signals of hunger and satiety. In addition, it promotes the development of a healthy relationship with food. If he does not finish his plate, do not force him to eat more. Do not use food as a reward, punishment, or as a bargain — your role in being a model a guide first and foremost. Consume with interest, curiosity, and enthusiasm the food served and behave well in front of your child. Remember, you are part of the "optimal environment" around your kids.

Finally, the control of the amount of food should be up to the child. Trust him! Children are intuitive eaters by default!

Chapter 14:
Intuitive Eating
FAQs

What happens when you learn an intuitive diet? The first stage is to achieve a dietary bottom - the situation when there is a distinct sensation: I will never go on a diet again. This is the moment when we can reject the rules that oppressively and very critically guided our diet. Gradually, awareness of nutrition begins to increase.

The next step is very often described by intuitive eaters as a bit strange. When everything is a little too much, too much attention is paid to food, sensations become too meaningful. At this point, jumps often occur. Sometimes failures, sometimes, on the contrary, everything is fine. This is a normal state of mastering new skills.

Next is the stage of awakening food intuition. Sensations become more accurate. You no longer confuse physiological hunger with anything else. Saturation also becomes understandable and meaningful. Gradually, there is a decrease in the concentration on food. You are no longer asking yourself a million questions about what and when to eat. The process is slightly automated. The next stage is considered the stage of confidence in the body. This is a sense of self-competence in the skills that you master, a decrease in self-criticism. The final stage is the pleasure of following your body, its needs. You do not use food as comfort, reward, or punishment. This is the level of trust in your body when you can allow yourself to no longer depend on external information flows and comments. Nobody can bring you down from your inner sense of self-confidence.

What if I have an underlying medical condition or allergy?
Often, the choice of food that is prohibited for any medical reason is associated with a particular dish. For example, you want a marmalade. It is understood that it is made using sugar. You need to try a replacement that does not cause an allergic reaction. It is unlikely that, in this case, you want pure sugar. The lack of reaction will show the range in which you can practice and make your choices.

Is intuitive nutrition expensive?
Simply put, no, it isn't. While you may think that in the long run, you will eat more; on the other hand, the reverse is the case. Once you start to understand your hunger signals and body cues, you spend less and less on foods and feeding.

What if I cannot stop after allowing myself to be indulged in all types of foods?

The first stage of mastering the skills of intuitive nutrition is the development of such a physical sensation as hunger, increasing its awareness. Then comes the legalization and reconciliation with food, and then the assimilation of satiety skills. One way is to literally say "Stop" to yourself and put your hand on the stomach, ask yourself how full you are.

Follow these rules, and you will be just fine.

What if I am a person who never gets tired of sweets?

When legalizing sweets, you must follow the rules. What does sweet mean to you? What do you focus on when choosing such products? Is it the desired taste, or do you want to feel some sensation in the body? What is now associated with sweets? Sometimes food becomes the most affordable way to feel that it is still your body.

If the brain requires sweets, it means that it knows something about how it affects you. By asking yourself what your need is, you can identify the true reason for the desire for sweets. After all, if there is no physiological hunger, food cannot satisfy a real need. That short-term effect will still give way to a real experience that will come subsequently from the inability to satisfy a true need.

Chapter 15:
Practical Guide to
Action

Managing your condition requires balance and wisdom. The stimulus that is associated with the physiological state and triggers it is called an anchor in the psychology of neurolinguistic programming. An anchor is all that causes an emotional state. Examples of naturally acting positive anchors are favorite photographs, smells, evocative words, and the tone of voice of a loved one. An anchor for you is the temptation of the tastes of products, the feeling of food.

Destruction of anchors

In order to destroy the anchors, you "anchor," that is,
as clearly as possible, you draw in your imagination an

undesirable negative state and an alluring positive state. These two anchors are turned on simultaneously. After a short mixing period, the negative state will change, and a new state will arise. This process can be understood so that the nervous system tries to turn on two incompatible conditions at the same time. It cannot do this, so it does something else. The old stereotype is destroyed, and the new one is created. Anchors make experiences accessible to conscious control, using those natural processes that usually occur unconsciously.

Exercise

Therefore, as another preventive work, I would recommend doing the following exercise:

For a positive state, you choose to enjoy the taste of food and its unlimited quantity. For a negative anchor - an unpleasant feeling of fullness of the stomach, pain during and after vomiting, shame, fear, self- accusation. Now turn on your imagination both of these anchors simultaneously. Focus on the process and strengthen the action of both anchors. That is, imagine these two pictures as clearly as possible with all the channels of perception and accept your feelings.

Perhaps you will find other resources, turning inward, analyzing your past. Try to discover something pleasant in your childhood that will now serve as a resource for you to start a new life. Maybe the bike on which you learned to maintain balance will serve as the anchor, the memory of which will help to maintain balance even now. Well, you didn't immediately sit down and go, at first you studied and stuffed bumps in your head! You are experiencing the whole process again now, but you are learning not to drive a bicycle, but yourself.

In general, childhood memories can open up unprecedented hidden in the subconscious and unfulfilled dreams. In childhood, we directly and easily dreamed that we would become actresses or outstanding stars, great pilots, etc. Unique childlike spontaneity will not accept these arguments on faith and will be a thousand times right! Now, you should like the children who learn first of all to love themselves and believe in themselves all their lives.

Go back even further, perhaps at a time when you only learned to distinguish between uppercase letters and lowercase letters, and then - to make words from letters, and at the same time realize that the meaning of words is determined not by the letters themselves, but by their order in the word. From words you learned to make sentences, and from sentences - paragraphs. In the same way, you learn to understand your feelings. At first, you may not know what this or that feeling means, but gradually their meaning will become clear. And all together, these feelings are summarized in sentences and paragraphs that make up your biography, your health, and your life. Listen to yourself, to your feelings - and they will show you the way to your own truth, to yourself.

Keep and protect these feelings; they lead you. It is possible that with age, they change somewhat, take on a new meaning. It is possible that some feelings from childhood have remained somewhere far away, but you can return to them now or create new ones, allow yourself to dream, and realize your dreams!

Recognizing your feelings (and if you want, recognizing the prompts of emotional eating) can be learned through introspection. Of course, the desire to be honest and the ability to be so are not the same things. Very often, a person is unable to conform to this ideal.

At the initial stage, as an episodic self-training for psychoanalysis, I propose to follow your emotions and conditions, leading to tonus tension of the muscles of the body, i.e., stress. You need to learn to identify the true cause of induced states and take measures to eliminate or mitigate it, as an unsatisfactory state of the psyche leads to a breakdown, namely to "gluttony."

"What was the occasion?" - The main question of today, requiring an answer. If the reason is revealed, we can learn a lot about what kind of experience or event poses a threat or insult to us and what unconscious reactions it causes. The very first such unconscious reaction will be thought with the taste of food, then it will turn into a visual image, gradually, with an increase in desire. And here the excitement and obsession reach the mark "Start! To the refrigerator! " Why? What was the reason for this reaction? Maybe scroll back to the tape and try to figure it out before this mechanism is launched? This is the same analytical work that I wrote about above.

Finding yourself under the guise of various roles is not an easy task, but having solved it, you will discover your true "I," your real desires and dreams. You will gain self- confidence, independence and you will find a lot of interesting things in your new life.

In general, such a thing as introspection helps to cope with any emotional problems when you can identify the cause of these problems. The purpose of my book is not to describe all the existing methods for maintaining your psychological health, but to make you want to do it yourself, find for yourself what you need.

Happiness is awareness of growth
The body is an energy system; it fully interacts energetically with the environment. I hope you know about it. In addition to the energy obtained by burning food, a person improves his energy tone or accumulates energy in contact with positive forces, such as a sunny clear day, a beautiful landscape, a meeting with a happy person ... All this has a stimulating effect, namely: the stronger you are charged with positive energies, all the more resistant to negative influences, and the "unique" ability to seize the problem. The more energetic your body, the more significant you are in this world.

If you are an emotional person, and at this stage of life for some reason, you have likewise emotionally close people for contacts, then you can sublimate these contacts for a while into communication with nature, art. Finally, go to the hairdresser, shop, beauty salon, just chat with a hairdresser or manicurist. And only you take a step towards the missing part in your life with both communication and making new contacts. You will be surprised, but they already exist for you; you just walked past them without noticing.

Have you forgotten about the emotional significance of communicating with your family? Or is the reason for the breakdown precisely because the emotional sphere in the family has weakened? Very often, this is the case. True? Well then, of course, it's not worth it to resist, it's up to you! Choose. Look for and eliminate unhealthy aspects in the emotional body so that they do not provoke the physical body to fail.

And further. And how much time do you devote to your inner world? Reflections, dreams, plans for the future, relaxation, meditation, listening to your favorite music, reading your favorite literature ... I would even call it "withdrawal into yourself." "What are your dreams? There is so much work that there's no time to rest, even if only for a good night's sleep! "- is there such an attitude? If yes, and you consider all this insignificant and frivolous to devote time to this, then take your emotional eating as a diagnosis, and as a means to improve your life. It is quite obvious that wallowing in the abyss of daily problems; you reduce attention to your inner self. Activity, career, development - this is very good. This is welcome.

But the crisis will come again in order to remind you: how do you love yourself, do you have enough rest, what's on your mental plane? After all, its goal is to make of you a particle harmoniously interacting with the Universe, a perfect Planet. After all, you yourself so strived for excellence! Or was there no such order and the universe was mistaken, sending you emotional eating? As you see, it's completely unprofitable for you to reduce your life to mechanical processes such as: "home - work," "slept - ate," "ate, and again the same thing," where is the development? Where is life itself?

Grow above yourself, knowing yourself and scooping infinite resources for happiness not from anywhere, but from yourself - this was my personal discovery!

Fears, stresses, troubles

One way or another, but in life, we have always been surrounded by fears, troubles, problems, stresses. I got nervous at work - of course, this is stress. Money was stolen - why not be upset? Broke your phone? Children do not obey? Nothing to wear and so on and so forth.

There are plenty of reasons for a bad mood, from dissatisfaction with life to deep psychological traumas, stressful conditions, and depression. And even more, we can invent them for ourselves and in all the richness of our imagination paint with all the colors of the rainbow. Our fears entail a whole series of disappointments, troubles, poor health, and disbelief.

What are we afraid of?

Around us is the unknown. We know this as a fact, as a given (only a few people are among the soothsayers who can look into the Universe). We do not need this. We need to identify what this internal fear and faith are. In whom, what? What is so bad in it and so good in it?

Fear arises precisely because of the unknown, we want to know the future and believe in it, hoping that it will certainly be good. But since we do not know it, we begin to fear in advance the troubles that could happen to us. We are subconsciously afraid to see ourselves in this future as sick, poor, desperate, insecure. Therefore, a fairly common way of self-torture is the ability to take and question the arrival of a beautiful future in advance. Or do it like this: "Now I'm better to get sick, suffer, be afraid - and work out my groundwork for the future, so as not to hurt and suffer there."

If we consider this scale as a horizontal thermometer, then as the "temperature" of passing certain feelings and sensations increases, we come to faith - faith in your bright future. So, we believe more in ourselves and in our strengths. So is there any point in doubting and fearing the future if the unknown is still on all sides? But on which side of the "thermometer" to live and perceive the troubles and failures in life - we can choose for ourselves!

And look, what an interesting picture it turns out if you converted your fear into faith in the future. Immediately with respect to another vertical vector, physical well- being improves, and health improves. And most importantly - you just start to grow on yourself! Through calm and poise, interest comes to life, its laws.

Improving well-being gives strength to the search in development. Cognition brings wisdom and peace. Confidence in the future gives the highest virtue - self- discipline. And finally, when you gain faith, you gain happiness, the ability to enjoy life, and become a self- sufficient person.

Since our fears are a product of our own imagination, then, accordingly, for balance, you can come up with any positive events and emotions that give pleasure and confidence in the future. It happens that there is no real danger, and fear or stress arises.

We can provide ourselves with positive emotions in the same way, and not wait until something good comes or comes. Why wait? All good things can be created here and now! Therefore, take this scheme as a plan - a guide to action, a simple mathematical algorithm for rebuilding your state from stress because of fear into a state of peace and faith in the future.

Unclear? Well then, an example: you are extremely annoyed and cause a number of unpleasant sensations by the new secretary of the boss. Now, you have to not only finish all the work but also make coffee for the guests. Besides, the girl really likes to smoke. But since she's "someone's daughter" and arguing with the leadership about the appropriateness at the workplace she occupies is a very ungrateful thing, I offer the following options for consideration.

1. You can be proud of your grip and ability to quickly cope not only with your work but also with her, too - and with pleasure to continue to work for two.

2. You can come to terms with this situation, reassuring yourself with the thought that that the girl will still learn and become more skilled, share her experience in the end.

3. You can discuss your responsibilities with the director and not exceed the "permissible" limit, even if you really want to finish everything about her.

4. You can philosophically relate to the issue because everything in this world is temporary and transient. You, with your experience, can find a place for yourself anywhere, but the poor girl is unlikely to stay in a reputable company without her "daddy" helping her.

5. And, finally, you can just change jobs, believing in yourself and not being afraid for your future, if only stress and tension do not arise.

In general, any situation can be accepted with love and self-interest.

Yes, this also works, a kind of building your own comfortable life and well-being. But only in this way can you work on your fears and not get depressed moving on to "binges," "bouts," and other negative activities. The main thing is to engage in positive activities.

I believe you can, and I wish you all the best in your endeavor!

Conclusion

Here came the moment of parting, and I need to say something in the end.

While you read this book, I was there, trying to guide you, answer your questions, support your legitimate desire to live better and be better in you. And I don't need more reward and appreciation for my work than the realization that my experience, transferred to paper, was useful to you too.

Perhaps some points remained abstract due to certain generalizations designed for different persons with their own nuances in the problem. However, I sincerely hope that I have given quite balanced answers to your most important questions.

The main thing that I wanted to talk about with you is about your current life. About how you want to lookand eat, how you want to relate to yourself and to people, how you plan to build your life in general, what changes to make based on the experience gained in your problem, and how to benefit and learn from it.

I hope my book has helped you rethink a lot and make your own decisions and new tactics of behavior, and not just food. Now you yourself can give an answer to the main question: "So what is it all the same for you – emotional eating?" Ordinary gluttony called human weakness? A malicious diagnosis that stigmatizes all life and from which there is no escape, except for lifelong treatment and the "degree of disability"? Or is it a stage on the path to a new life, a tool that opens your eyes to both yourself and the whole world around you?"

Does it still look so unacceptable and inhumane, as you used to consider it? Or does it have its own rational grains? When you pose such direct questions to yourself and honestly answer them, a pleasant realization comes that everything is in your hands, no matter how trite these words would sound. Only I would change the meaning of this line with only one pronoun: "Listen, everything is in your hands, yes, YOU!" Of course, we all understand that we live our own lives and are, to one degree or another, the masters of our own destiny, we all crave love and respect for ourselves and quite rightly believe that we deserve it. But when problems and diseases come to life, we usually ask one question: "For what?"

In man, everything is created for enjoyment, and not for extermination or constant remaking. Take without any regard the enjoyment of your life, your choice, your body, your business, environment, family, and people around you. It's all your choice, and it's up to you, with love, care, and gratitude, to accept all this or to reject, tear yourself out of a great society.

Believe in yourself; you are the best and worthy of all the blessings and pleasures that the Universe keeps for you! Take advantage, love, and be loved!

CPSIA information can be obtained
at www.ICGtesting.com
Printed in the USA
BVHW092107180321
602886BV00004B/872

9 781914 136481